AN INTRODUCTION TO

GREEK PHILOSOPHY

J.V. LUCE

THAMES AND HUDSON

© 1992 Thames and Hudson Ltd, London
Reprinted 1997

ISBN 0-500-27655-2

Printed and bound in Slovenia by Mladinska Knjiga

CONTENTS

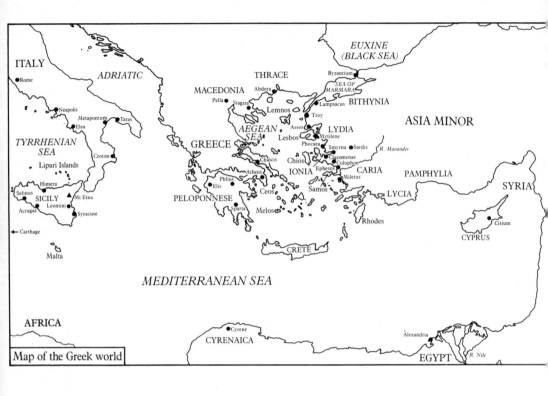

Map of the Greek world

PREFACE

THE AIM OF this book is to provide a concise account of the course of Greek philosophy from its first beginnings in Ionia in the sixth century BC down to the emergence of Neoplatonism in the third century AD. I have tried to present the facts in a way that will be intelligible to readers with no knowledge of Greek and no previous acquaintance with philosophy.

The interpretation of the source material, particularly for the earlier thinkers, is often highly controversial. In such cases I have not attempted to argue out disputed views in detail, but have plumped for the line of interpretation which seemed to me most plausible. A brief account of the Sources is provided at the end of the Introduction, and Suggestions for Further Reading can be found at the back of the book.

Some readers may feel that there is too much biographical detail, but many of the ancient philosophers were remarkable personalities, and I believe it is valuable to try to see them as individuals in a particular social context. In order to define this context more fully I have included some account of the main historical events that affected the course of philosophy, notably the early flowering of the Ionian city-states, their conquest by the Persians which led to a westward dispersion of philosophical ideas, and the successful counter-attack by Alexander the Great that initiated the Hellenistic Age.

A glossary of some key Greek philosophical terms is given in an Appendix. Such terms are italicised and marked with an asterisk on their first occurrence in the text. The translations of source material are my own unless otherwise attributed.

7

My debts to previous treatments are too numerous to acknowledge, but I wish to express my grateful thanks to my colleague Professor J. C. A. Gaskin who kindly read the whole work in draft and made many helpful suggestions for its improvement. To the sound judgement and patient encouragement of my wife I owe, as always, more than I can say.

Trinity College   J. V. LUCE
Dublin

INTRODUCTION

GREEK PHILOSOPHY originated early in the sixth century BC in the prosperous and progressive Ionian city-state of Miletus. From these small but daringly innovative beginnings the movement eventually spread all over the ancient world, maintaining its creativity for upwards of a thousand years. Over this long period it displayed many widely different veins of thought, ranging from science to mysticism, from idealism to materialism, from dogmatism to scepticism. Yet the subject also exhibits a remarkable inner coherence in that each successive phase appears as the natural and logical outcome of what had gone before. Foreign influences were minimal. Greek philosophy has a good claim to be regarded as the most original and influential achievement of the Greek genius.

It is impossible to over-emphasise its pervasive effect on subsequent European thought. The whole fabric of Western culture is still deeply coloured by its assumptions, methods, and terminology. Atomic theory and ethics, mathematics and logic, metaphysics and theology, are more than just ancient Greek words. They are key modern ways of ordering experience and comprehending reality, and they remain closely patterned on their original models.

To the ancient Greeks the pursuit of philosophy was an all-embracing pursuit of knowledge about the world which also involved an understanding of man's place in it. After an initial and rapid phase of growth lasting about two centuries, philosophy achieved a dominant position in higher education, and thereafter provided millions with guidance and inspiration for the conduct of their lives. The seminal opening phase, known as the Presocratic period, lasted from c.600–400BC. Philosophical thinking was then consolidated by Plato and Aristotle and the teaching schools which they founded in Athens in the fourth century BC. The period after

9

Socrates centred round these and other schools, and ran on without any marked break down to AD529, when, in the interests of Christianity, the Emperor Justinian ordered their closure.

In the Presocratic period the main thrust of enquiry was directed towards achieving a rational understanding of the external world of nature. Speculation was dominated by large questions about the origin of the world, the number and nature of its constituent parts, the difference between appearance and reality, and the problem of how movement and change could be reconciled with the concept of permanent substance. In response to the disagreements which soon emerged, formal techniques of argument and refutation began to be developed. Some of the thinkers were driven to reflect on the nature of knowledge itself as distinct from opinion or perception. The period culminated in the elaboration of an atomic theory of material substance. It also saw the beginnings of philosophical sects, notably the brotherhood of thinkers founded by Pythagoras (*c.*570–*c.*495BC). Early Pythagoreanism was the milieu in which philosophy first became a way of life as well as a discipline of intellectual enquiry.

From our modern standpoint the Presocratic thinkers look more like scientists than philosophers, and many of their problems would now be handled under separate sciences like physics, astronomy or meteorology. But they should not be dislodged from their traditional position as the founding fathers of Greek philosophy as a whole. At this early stage there was as yet no clear distinction between different types of intellectual enquiry. Various thinkers deployed the methods of observation, of mathematics, and of logical argument in the single task of reaching a comprehensive understanding of the essential nature of the universe. If one is looking for a label for their work, 'natural philosophy' is perhaps the best. The Presocratics displayed an epoch-making confidence in the power of human reason to unravel the essence of things. The heart of their achievement lay in their determined search for simple and all-embracing explanations, and in their development of the concept of a world order with a pattern accessible to the human mind.

The contribution of Socrates (469–399BC) gave a decisive new turn to the development of the subject. He lost interest in the attempts of earlier thinkers to explain the natural world, and began to stress the supreme importance of what he called 'expertise in human nature'. He advocated a critical examination of one's way of life with a view to establishing a true scale of values based on reason rather than tradition. His influence on his followers, including Plato (427–347BC), was so strong that ethical considerations now became, and remained, a central preoccupation of all subsequent Greek philosophy.

Plato and Aristotle (384–322BC) both made major contributions to the development of ethical and political thought. But they also maintained the impetus of scientific enquiry through the teaching and research activities of their schools. Plato's Academy was particularly noted for its contributions to mathematics and astronomy, and Aristotle's Lyceum for progress in zoology and botany. Remarkable advances were also made in the development of philosophy in the narrower sense in which the word is now generally used. These included the working-out of techniques of dialectic and logic, acute and penetrating discussion of the nature of knowledge and how it is attained, and the elaboration of metaphysical concepts.

Systematisation of thought was perhaps the leading characteristic of the centuries after Socrates. Plato and Aristotle set the trend by developing formal curricula of instruction in their schools, and the fashion was followed in the long-lived and highly influential schools of Stoicism and Epicureanism which were established *c.*300BC. These two schools emerged at the time when the older Greek world of the city-states had been transformed by Alexander the Great's conquest and annexation of the Persian Empire. With the establishment of Greek imperial rule in Egypt, Asia Minor, and Syria, Greek influence spread widely through the Near East. The Hellenistic Age, as it is called, spanned a period of some three centuries from 323 to 31BC. The Greeks were then militarily and culturally dominant from the Eastern Mediterranean to the Persian Gulf. The study of Greek philosophy permeated the area, and in the second century BC its influence began to be felt as far west as Rome, where Stoic ethics in particular took a powerful hold among the Roman upper classes.

The educational role and intellectual standing of Greek philosophy was not affected by the eastward expansion of Rome and the Roman take-over of the Hellenistic kingdoms. Platonism and Aristotelianism continued to mould the shape of metaphysics, and Stoicism and Epicureanism were potent influences in the conduct of life.

If you disliked the dogmatism of the major schools you could become a Sceptic. Scepticism was a minor but philosophically significant school which also emerged early in the Hellenistic period. The Sceptics challenged the dogmatic certainties of their rivals, recommending suspension of judgement as the only prudent course in an uncertain and unknowable world. In particular, they tried to undermine confidence in the evidence of the senses, deploying a well-developed series of arguments relating to illusion, many of which are still current coin in modern discussions of sense perception.

The idealistic vein in Greek thought deriving from Pythagoras and Plato began to regain prominence in the first century AD, and eventually culminated in that eloquent re-affirmation of higher values which we call Neoplatonism. Neoplatonism was a creative synthesis of previous speculations about the nature and destiny of man's immortal soul and the paramount reality of the unseen world of immaterial form and transcendent spirit. As a system it was established by Plotinus (AD204–270) at Rome in the middle of the third century AD. Plotinus looked to Plato for his inspiration, but went beyond the Platonic dialogues in his eloquent portrayal of the divine world of the Intellect.

Thus Greek philosophy, which began as an attempt to understand the world without recourse to religious myth, ended up as a rational theology which attempted to define in detail the relationship between God, the soul, and the world. In a way the wheel of thought had come full circle. It would, however, be a mistake, in my opinion, to regard Greek philosophy as having originated in conscious opposition to Greek religion. Greek religion was fundamentally a matter of cult rather than creed, and its intellectual content was never high. The various gods and goddesses were regarded as powerful and capricious spirits, able to help, and prone to harm mankind. Common prudence required their propitiation with traditional rituals of prayer and sacrifice. The poets did something to raise the tone. The majesty of Zeus was enhanced by the poetic imagination of Homer, and his justice was extolled by Hesiod and Aeschylus, but non-philosophical Greek literature never attained the spiritual insights of the Jewish Old Testament writers. In popular conception the Olympians remained an unpredictable family of invisible beings exercising an arbitrary and far from moral sway over hapless mortals.

Greek philosophy was in no way indebted to Greek polytheism. It was rather the case that the religious consciousness of Greece was enhanced by her philosophers. This process is particularly clear in Plato and Aristotle. Plato wanted to refine religion, not reject it, and so he combined stringent criticism of the traditional stories about the gods with a reasoned presentation of the divine nature as totally honest and benevolent in word and deed. Aristotle's extraordinary achievement in theology was to deduce an elevated and monotheistic view of deity from the nature of the physical world.

The theme of the interaction between religious belief and philosophy is just one of a number of themes which are developed in what follows. If the reader is interested in tracing a particular theme rather than studying individual thinkers he or she should find help in the Index. The story of Greek philosophy is wide-ranging and complex, and I proceed next to give a brief outline of the sources on which any account must be based.

A NOTE ON THE SOURCES

The study of Greek philosophy is based on three main types of source:

(1) Complete texts
Only Plato, Aristotle, and Plotinus can be read in this way. The thought of all other major philosophers has to be reconstructed from sources (2) and (3).

(2) Fragments (quotations)
Most Greek philosophical texts survive only in 'fragments', a collective term for quotations preserved in later writers. The 'fragments' amount to only a very small proportion of the originals, but gain in significance because they tend to illustrate the more striking or novel aspects of their authors' thought.

(A) Fragments from the Presocratic period (c.600–400BC)
The sources here extend from Plato in the fourth century BC to Simplicius in the sixth century AD. Simplicius produced a well-informed, and still extant, commentary on Aristotle's *Physics*, which contains extensive excerpts from the Presocratics. His help is

13

invaluable in reconstructing the thought of Anaximander, Parmenides, Anaxagoras and Zeno.

Plutarch in his *Moralia* (second century AD) has hundreds of quotations, and the early Christian writers Clement of Alexandria (*c*.AD150–215) and Hippolytus of Rome (*c*.AD170–236) are also very useful sources.

For guidance in finding these and other fragments, both in Greek and in translation, the reader is referred to the Suggestions for Further Reading section.

(B) Fragments of the Stoics and Epicureans
The founders of Stoicism were voluminous writers, but their works are extant only in scattered fragments. Epicurus too was a prolific author — he is credited with 300 rolls — but these, including his thirty-seven 'books' on the nature of the world, have largely perished, a small proportion only surviving in some badly charred papyri from Herculaneum. For the rest we have three doctrinal letters by him (one possibly not authentic), two collections of maxims, and beyond that only fragments.

(C) Fragments (and expositions) in Latin
Passages translated from the Greek originals are sometimes to be found in Latin writers. We may also turn to them for a reasonably coherent picture of Stoicism, notably in the philosophical writings of Cicero (106–43BC) (who is a major source for all the Hellenistic Schools), and in the Roman Stoics, Seneca (*c*.5BC–AD65) and Marcus Aurelius (AD121–180). A most impressive presentation of Epicureanism is given by Lucretius (*c*.99–55BC) in his great philosophical poem *De Rerum Natura*.

(3) The doxographical tradition

(A) For the Presocratics
A 'doxographer' means one who collected and commented on the opinions (*doxai**) of others, so the 'doxographical tradition' embodies what is left of the ancient Greek attempt to trace the history of their own philosophy.

The tradition basically stems from the work of Aristotle and his School. Aristotle was the first philosopher to make a systematic

---

*All terms marked with an asterisk are defined in the Glossary on pp.162–5.

study of his predecessors, quoting and criticising them, and often prefacing his treatises with a summary account of the evolution of previous thought in that particular field of study.

A more comprehensive treatment was provided by his pupil Theophrastus (*c.*372–286BC) in his general history of Presocratic thought. This ran to sixteen (or eighteen) books, and was entitled *Opinions of the Physicists*. Theophrastus used an analytical approach, setting out the various opinions under general headings such as the gods, the soul, the heavenly bodies, the earth, and so on. He also wrote special studies of some major figures, none of which has survived. The bulk of the general work has also perished, with the exception of most of the last book, which dealt with Sensation, and some important extracts from the first book on Material Principles preserved by Simplicius.

Great light was thrown on the many ramifications of the doxographical tradition by the pioneering work of H. Diels (1879), and subsequent studies have helped to firm up our understanding of its complexities. The results of this modern research are well set out in the general histories of Burnet, and of Kirk, Raven, and Schofield, to which the reader is referred for further details.

(B) For Socrates, Plato, and later philosophers

The most comprehensive later manifestation of the doxographical tradition is to be found in an extant work in ten books entitled *Lives of Eminent Philosophers* by Diogenes Laertius (probably dating from the first half of the third century AD). Diogenes deals with the lives and doctrines of all the major philosophers from Thales to Epicurus, naming as his sources over 200 authors and 300 works. Diogenes was not an acute thinker. Nietzsche called him 'the nightwatchman of Greek philosophy, guarding treasure whose value he did not comprehend'. He was at best an industrious compiler, and his work is very uneven in quality, but our knowledge would be considerably the poorer had his *Lives* not survived.

There is also extant an important collection of writings by Sextus Empiricus (perhaps *c.*AD200). Sextus was a doctor by profession, a sceptical philosopher in his own right, and a much keener thinker than Diogenes. His writings relate primarily to the history of Scepticism, which formally dates back to Pyrrho in the fourth century BC, but they also contain significant information about other philosophical systems early and late.

1

THE BIRTH OF PHILOSOPHY
IN IONIA

THE REGION ANCIENTLY called Ionia is the one of the most beautiful and well-favoured areas on the surface of this planet. It covered
what is now the central portion of the western sea-board of Turkey,
stretching from the Gulf of Smyrna in the north to the valley of the
Maeander in the south, a distance of about 100 miles (160 kilometres) in all. With its bold promontories and large off-shore
islands the land provides a well-varied blend of mountain and plain,
rich in pasture and tillage, and interspersed with orchards and olive
groves. Winters are mild, with abundant rainfall. Copious springs
and large perennial rivers help to maintain greenery through the
heat of summer. There is no better climate in the whole world. Put a
gifted people in this environment, and allow them to take root, and
they were bound to prosper.

   The initial Greek settlement of Ionia dates back to the collapse of
the Mycenaean world towards the end of the twelfth century BC.
Refugees from mainland Greece then began to filter eastwards
across the Aegean in small detachments, seeking a new home for
themselves in the western fringes of Asia Minor. During the course
of the next few centuries the whole region became thoroughly
Hellenised, and by the end of the seventh century twelve of the
original Ionian settlements had evolved into prosperous and progressive city-states, each politically independent, but all of them
co-operating in a loosely knit federation known as the Ionian
League. Most of the urban centres of the League were thriving
sea-ports, quick to adopt new ideas like the recent invention of
coined money by their eastern neighbour Lydia. They were also in
the forefront of the development of the city-state system itself.

Nothing like the *polis* — I use the Greek name for a typically Greek thing — had been seen in the world before. In outward form it was the walled centre of a small independent state. But in spirit it was a community of free citizens associating freely under a constitution of their own devising. The Greeks had realised that political freedom could only be achieved under the rule of law, and the development of Greek literacy from the eighth century on gave them an important new tool for achieving their goal. 'Law-givers' were key figures in the evolution of the *polis* all over the Greek world, and the laws they promulgated were published in written form accessible to all the citizens. The Ionians were quick to respond to these advances. Already by *c.*650 the people of Chios had inscribed their constitution on a stone pillar (which was found in the south of the island in 1907). The most significant phrase on it is 'The People's Council', which shows that the Chiots were already some distance down the road to democracy.

The Ionian city-states were tiny by our standards, but their quality of life was high. In artistic achievement, commercial practice, and constitutional organisation, they were in the van of human progress. They had the good fortune to be left alone to develop for some centuries without any serious threat from a foreign imperial power. Their position on the eastern limits of the Greek world was a favourable one for trade with the Orient, and also for stimulating contact with non-Greek peoples. Most important of all was the state of mind produced by their history and situation. They were colonists and so less hide-bound by tradition. They had the leisure and opportunity to travel and to indulge their curiosity about the world. They were free men, subservient neither to king nor priest, and it was clear to them that their prosperity was largely the result of their own enterprise and effort. All this gave them a forward-looking self-confidence which was a crucial precondition for intellectual advance.

Nowhere was the interplay of all these factors more intense than in the great harbour city of Miletus. Founder of numerous colonies, chiefly in the Pontic regions to the north, Miletus was an important manufacturing centre, and also an emporium for the goods of Anatolia and the Aegean. Her merchant ships ranged all over the Mediterranean and the Black Sea, and she maintained close commercial ties with Egypt. It was here in the early decades of the sixth century that thought about the world struggled out of its cocoon of myth and fable, and began to try out its wings in the free air of philosophical speculation.

The Milesian School comprised three great thinkers, Thales, Anaximander, and Anaximenes, whose lives span the period from *c.*625 to 525. They were not a 'school' in the formal institutional sense that later became current, but the term is applicable to them because they shared a common interest in the natural world, and tried to understand and explain it in a rational way. They were all natives of the same city, and they must all have been known to each other. The doxographical tradition is unanimous in maintaining that they 'heard' each other, and therefore presumably learnt from each other, in succession.

THALES

Life and activities

Thales became famous throughout Greece as the chief representative of the 'Seven Wise Men', a group 'canonised' for their practical wisdom and statesmanship rather than for philosophy in our sense of the word. The group included men who are known to have been politically active early in the sixth century, and this was also true of Thales. The ancient chronologists put his prime (his fortieth year) at *c.*585, and we shall not be far wrong if we date his life from *c.*625 to *c.*545. It is far from clear whether he left anything in writing, and even if he did, not a single certain fragment survives.

In Thales's day Miletus was a central point in world trade. It would have been natural for one of its leading citizens to take an interest in the expertise of the non-Greek world, and there is evidence that he did so. He appears to have known something of Babylonian astronomy and Phoenician navigational methods, and he is said to have made solar observations to determine the length of the periods between solstice and equinox. He is also said to have calculated the height of the pyramids in Egypt by the neat device of waiting for the moment in the day when his own shadow was equal to his height, and then pacing out the shadow cast by the monuments.

This report is part of a wider tradition that Thales brought 'geometry' from Egypt to Greece. The priests and scribes in ancient Egypt had developed some skill in elementary triangulation at a much earlier date than Thales, and they put their knowledge to practical use in calculating the angles in pyramid construction, and in re-surveying for taxation purposes fields that had been obliterated by Nile floods. Such skills would have been of interest to the enquiring mind of a visiting Greek, and it is quite possible that Thales was the first to acquire and relay this knowledge back to his homeland. The subsequent achievement of Greek mathematicians was to incorporate this Egyptian knowledge into the structured system of propositions which we call 'geometry' (which by derivation means 'land measurement'). Thales was credited with starting this process by discovering some elementary theorems, for example, that a circle is bisected by its diameter, and that the angles at the base of an isosceles triangle are equal. However, it is on the whole more likely that such theorems were merely implicit in some of the mensuration carried out by Thales, and that explicit proof of them came later.

So far the picture of Thales that emerges from the sources is that of a man who was actively involved in the political and commercial concerns of his city, and whose enquiring mind was also keenly engaged in the attempt to understand and master his environment. He was all of this, but he must have been something more to gain his title as the founder of philosophy.

The eclipse

His single most famous exploit was to predict that a solar eclipse would occur in the course of a given year. The prediction came true, and the event was particularly remembered because the eclipse took place on a day when the Lydians and the Medes were about to do battle. The date of this eclipse has been established as 28 May 585, a crucial date for Thales's life, and an even more crucial date for science. Those who like anniversaries can justly celebrate it as the birthday of natural philosophy.

Assuming that the prediction was made (and it is well attested), one must go on to ask how Thales did it. By observations extending over many centuries the Babylonians had established that eclipses of the sun and moon tend to repeat themselves after a cycle of 223 lunar months — the so-called Saros cycle. The cycle spans just over eighteen years, and there had been an eclipse of the sun in Egypt in 603, which is eighteen years before 585. If Thales had seen, or heard of, the eclipse in Egypt, and known of the Saros cycle, he could easily have put two and two together, and risked his prediction. Data of this sort can only indicate that there will *probably* be a solar eclipse visible *somewhere* on the earth's surface. If Thales was relying on Babylonian data, his luck was in.

But the method of his prediction is of less significance than the mental attitude revealed by it. Thales, in effect, was placing his confidence in the uniformity of nature, a confidence doubtless based on his own, as well as other people's, astronomical observations. He must have sensed that there was a regular pattern underlying the occurrence of eclipses, and must have accepted that they depended on the orderly movements of the heavenly bodies, not on the capricious and unpredictable will of a god. This was an epoch-making change of attitude. Less than a century before, the Ionian poet Archilochus had reacted very differently after viewing a solar eclipse: 'Anything can happen — Zeus has darkened the sun at noon.' Like Archilochus, the Medes and Lydians were dismayed by the eclipse of 585. They broke off the fighting and made peace. Thales had advanced beyond the stage of superstitious awe. He was trying to understand the event in terms of natural cycles.

The primacy of Water
The prediction alone would have made him a memorable figure. But Aristotle singled him out as the 'founder of natural philosophy' for a different reason. He reports him as having maintained that all things originate from Water. This 'supposition', according to Aristotle, implied that the *element* Water is the basic *substance* out of which everything in the world has originated and into which it will ultimately be resolved. Individual things come into existence and pass out of existence, but Water endures. Thales himself would not have used terms like 'element' and 'substance'. Aristotle is presenting (and, some would say, distorting) the essence of his thought in language forged by subsequent philosophical enquiry.

We do not know exactly how Thales phrased his new hypothesis. He may well have used the word *arche** ('beginning' or 'source') to characterise Water. But whatever the language, there is an unmistakable grandeur and novelty about the theory. Thales must have thought long and hard about water, and it is not hard to see the line his thought took. He thought about water as the source of life (semen is 'watery') and necessary to its continuance, about water solidifying into ice and vapourising into steam, about water surrounding the land masses, about water descending from the sky and welling up from the ground. Finally he reached out to the bold generalisation that 'All is Water'.

The cosmogonical myths of Egypt and Babylonia pictured a primordial waste of waters in existence before the emergence of any dry land. A similar notion underlies the biblical account of the Creation, according to which 'In the beginning...darkness was upon the face of the deep.' Thales, as has often been suggested, may have been acquainted with such myths, and may have gained hints for his thought from them. His belief that the stability of the earth was due to its floating on water has an obvious affinity with the account in Genesis of 'waters under the firmament', and may well be indebted to Near Eastern mythology. But it is worth noting that he makes a typically Greek use of the flotation concept to explain earthquakes. These he attributed to the occasional rolling of the earth on its watery bed like a ship in a storm at sea, a clear indication of the scientific bent of his mind.

Thales's originality lay in detaching the principle of the primacy of water from all mythological trappings, and in using it to provide natural explanations of natural events. This was a momentous intellectual insight that marked a decisive advance on all previously recorded speculations about the origin and nature of the world. The character of the advance becomes clear if one compares the poet Hesiod's account of such matters in his *Theogony*, composed about a century earlier. Hesiod's poem is an account of the birth of the gods, and is cluttered with a huge array of divine beings, including vast and vague primordial figures like Chaos, Erebos, and Night. His thought is dominated by theological considerations. Thales, by contrast, is recognisably a scientist, and his thought has a conceptual consistency not found in myths. He has seized on the essential notion that the world is not the product of divine couplings, as Hesiod proclaimed, but an entity existing in its own right with one basic 'nature' (*phusis**), a *watery* 'nature', which sustains the life of plants and animals.

The life-force

Just as Thales took a generalised view of water, so he probably took a generalised view of 'life'. There is some evidence that he speculated about a vital force present in contexts not obviously watery. He seems to have been impressed by the attraction of iron by the

21

'Magnesian stone' — a natural magnet — and also by the attractive powers of amber. Observation showed him that these apparently inanimate substances could induce movement in other things, and therefore, he seems to have argued, they must really be alive.

This line of thought may underlie his reported saying: 'All things are full of gods.' In this striking dictum he was, I believe, expressing a 'hylozoistic' view of the world, namely, that all 'matter' (*hule**) is imbued with 'life' (*zoe*). The inherent life of the natural world, he may have thought, was seen in its perpetual mobility, and in its more than human power to change and transform itself. To the Greek mind the distinguishing mark of a 'god' was unending life combined with perpetual activity. To Thales's eye the world itself exhibited these characteristics, and so it was natural for him to say that its constituent parts were 'full of gods'. His 'watery principle' fitted neatly into such speculations because water is inherently mobile, as well as obviously necessary for life.

Thales's world, then, was like a living organism, perpetually generated and nourished by water conceived as a vital fluid, permeating and activating all things. Such is the picture that seems to emerge from our scanty and second-hand sources. It must be emphasised that the detailed interconnections of his system as outlined above are largely inferential, and much depends on the interpretation of the cryptic saying about the ubiquity of 'gods'. This was not, I would maintain, a theological utterance, but a pithy saying by the first *phusikos**, that is to say the first thinker to propound a comprehensive account of the *phusis* of the world, based largely on his own observations and inferences. He seems to have outlined a daring and unified scheme of natural process, a scheme thought out along rational lines, which justly marks out its author as a major innovator in the history of human thought.

ANAXIMANDER

Life and writings

Anaximander, born in 610, was a younger contemporary of Thales. His dates rest on an unusually precise report that he was sixty-four years old in 546 and died soon afterwards. The year 546 was the date of a decisive moment in world history when the Persians under Cyrus captured Lydian Sardis and moved west to subdue Ionia.

These events meant the end of Ionian political independence, but they also initiated a fruitful dispersal of the Ionian genius, for many Ionians refused to accept the Persian yoke and went into voluntary exile. As a result the seeds of philosophy were soon broadcast all over the Greek world.

Like Thales, Anaximander played his part in the practical affairs of Miletus, leading one of its numerous colonising ventures. But he never achieved the widespread fame of Thales as a statesman. His forte was comprehensive intellectual enquiry, well symbolised by the fact that he was said on good authority to have been 'the first who dared to depict the inhabited world on a tablet'. Anaximander's world map would have been based on travellers' and sailors' information collected and correlated in Miletus.

There is no doubt that Anaximander committed his system to writing. He applied both his mind and his pen to the task of giving a rational account of the world, aiming to do this from its first beginnings down to the emergence of the human race on the surface of the earth. It was not customary for authors to provide titles at this early date, and Anaximander probably just began his work with a formula like: 'These are the words of Anaximander of Miletus.' But the later title of *On Nature*, under which his work circulated, was an appropriate one. The various extant summaries of his doctrines indicate a very comprehensive spread of interests, ranging from cosmogony and cosmology, through astronomy and meteorology, to the origins of animal and human life. A modern scientist might well object that he had neither the data nor the instruments for such an enterprise, but such considerations did not deter the speculative intellect of Anaximander. He applied his reason to the facts as he saw them, and came up with some brilliant hypotheses which still excite the admiration of historians of ideas. If Thales founded natural philosophy, Anaximander may be regarded as the originator of theoretical physics.

The *apeiron*
In his choice of a first principle on which to construct the world he in effect rejected Thales's view about the primacy of Water. He went back in thought behind the elemental masses of Fire, Air, Earth, and Water to something *indeterminate* which he described by the Greek term *apeiron**, which in general means 'boundless' or 'unlimited'.

It is by no means certain precisely how he understood the nature of this *apeiron*. He probably conceived of it as 'boundless' in the sense that it had no beginning or end in time, and he may also (though less certainly) have thought of it as infinitely extended in space. It is likely that he described it as the 'surround' of our world, regarding it, apparently, as an inexhaustible reservoir for the stuff of the visible world. So he probably conceived it as an indefinitely extended margin of formless material lying beyond the perceptible heavenly bodies.

Simplicius states explicitly that the *apeiron* was 'neither water nor any of the so-called elements'. This has been somewhat perversely taken to mean that the *apeiron* was actually all of them, but I follow the majority view that it was actually none of them. Thales's Water was wet, but Anaximander's basic stuff lacked all determinate qualities, being neither moist nor dry nor hot nor cold. This was perhaps the main reason why he posited it in the first place. There is evidence that he argued that if Water, or any other determinate stuff, were primary, it would be so dominant that no other element could come into being. Anaximander's *apeiron* was conceptually akin to the later definition of matter as 'something we know not what'. But it must have contained potentially, and in solution, as it were, the various characteristics of the elements that were later to form the basis of the world as we know it.

The cosmic vortex

Anaximander seems to have conceived of the process of world formation as due to a whirling motion operating within the *apeiron*. His thought here may have been guided by the observation of what happens when a vortex forms in water or air. The heavier materials in such a vortex tend to move to the centre and the lighter are deposited at the circumference. On a cosmic scale, this, to his mind, could have been the explanation of the fact that the centre of our world appears to be occupied by the heavy mass of the Earth, while the lighter elements such as Fire and Air have moved out to the circumference. There is reason to think that he used the term 'separating off' for this process, which resulted in the establishment of four major 'opposites': Hot, Cold, Moist, Dry. Following Aristotle we think of 'hot' and 'cold' as qualities or properties of substances, but such categorisation was foreign to the Milesian way of thinking. For Anaximander, Hot, Cold, Moist, and Dry were powers in their own right. Once the 'opposites' were separated off from the *apeiron* they had a natural tendency to interact like hostile forces, a tendency most obvious in the inability of Fire to coexist with Water.

World process and world order

Anaximander seems to have given a general explanation of world process as stemming from the inherent tendency of the primary 'opposites' to attempt to conquer one another. Such a principle would help to explain the annual alternation of the seasons. In winter 'cold' and 'wet' gain a temporary ascendancy. In summer the balance tilts in favour of 'hot' and 'dry'. Anaximander thought that in the nature of things no single 'opposite' is allowed to gain permanent ascendancy, for such dominance would destroy the balance of the universe. Thus world process is self-regulating, maintaining its rhythm by alternate swings in the direction of one extreme or another. The process proceeds under the impulse of the continued conflict between the 'opposites'.

We can read Anaximander's own formulation of this principle of a self-regulating balance of things in the one complete sentence preserved from his book. This precious quotation, the earliest extant fragment of Western philosophy-cum-science, runs as follows:

> Things render due recompense to one another for their injustice in accordance with the arrangement made by time.

As Simplicius remarks, the expression is 'rather poetical'. This is partly due to the use of the terms 'injustice' and 'recompense', which would normally be associated with human litigants rather than inanimate objects, and partly to the bold personification of time. But the thought behind the statement is clear enough. In the metaphor of 'injustice' Anaximander is expressing the idea of an undue advance or encroachment of one element upon another. If such an advance were allowed to continue unchecked, the world might become all fire or all water. But this does not happen because there is an inherent 'justice' in the nature of things which redresses the balance after the lapse of a given period of time. We use phrases like 'time heals', 'time renews', and the notion of the restorative power of time must form an important part of Anaximander's thought about world process. This is evident in the significant placing of the phrase 'the arrangement made by time' at the end of the sentence. The whole sentence expresses the faith of a physicist that the natural processes of our world are governed by an internal self-regulating mechanism that keeps the warring opposites in balance by making compensatory adjustments after the lapse of appropriate periods of time.

The shape and stability of the earth
Anaximander's view of the shape of the earth represents an interesting half-way stage between the primitive flat disc view and the sophisticated globe conception which was not reached by Greek thinkers until a generation or so later. He pictured the earth as a cylinder, comparing it to the drum of a column, and estimating that its depth was one third of its diameter.

But a much more remarkable advance in thought about the earth was his rejection of the need to provide any support for it. This was, in effect, another criticism of Thales, who supposed it to float on water, and who did not go on to ask what supported the water. An ancient summary of Anaximander's view runs as follows:

> The earth is aloft [that is, hangs freely in the surrounding air], not under any compulsion of forces, but remaining in position because it is equidistant from everything.

We can glimpse here the outline of a remarkable argument, in no way based on observation, but grounded entirely in theoretical considerations. Aristotle puts the nub of it in the concept of 'similarity'. We would probably use the term 'equilibrium'. The argument is that the earth, being centrally placed, and being equably related to the material surrounding it on all sides, has no reason or impulse to move in one direction rather than another. And since it cannot move in opposite directions simultaneously it has no option but to remain at rest.

The inadequacies of our sources have led to much dispute about most aspects of Anaximander's system, but despite the uncertainties he still looms through the fog of controversy as an intellectual colossus. With nothing except his own wit and the speculations of Thales to go on, he pioneered an astonishingly comprehensive account of the natural world. His conception of matter was daringly innovative and remained influential. Above all, his view of natural change as a balanced and self-regulating process controlled by time and necessity marked a radical break with all previous mythological accounts of the world's workings. The system of Anaximander and its promulgation in writing gave unmistakable notice that the rational approach inaugurated by Thales had now become a permanent feature of human intellectual endeavour.

ANAXIMENES

Life and writings

Anaximenes completes the great Milesian trio. Ancient tradition made him Anaximander's friend and philosophical 'successor', that is to say, pupil. No other details about his personal life have survived. The date of his birth was set *c*.585. If we accept that he was in his prime at the time of the Persian conquest in 546, he will have lived on for several decades in a generally subjugated Ionia. When he died we do not know.

Diogenes reports that his style was 'straightforward and plain', in deliberate contrast, perhaps, to the 'somewhat poetical' language of Anaximander. This implies that some writings of his survived at least to the Hellenistic period, but no titles have been preserved. Only one quoted sentence (probably a paraphrase) and some scattered phrases and words survive from his work.

System of nature: rarefaction and condensation

Anaximenes has been called a 'pallid reflection' of his great predecessor, and compared to a 'conventional scholar succeeding to an existing professorship'. These judgements seem over-harsh. It is true that his view of the world conforms to the general Milesian pattern, and that some of his theorising seems cautious, and even retrogressive, by comparison with Anaximander. But he made one important and far-reaching contribution to the analysis of physical process and change.

Anaximenes accepted that the world was to be explained in terms of the modifications of one primary or basic substance which must be infinite in extent. But he did not accept the primacy of Anaximander's unperceived 'indeterminate'. Instead he reverted to the attitude of Thales that one of the four elements must be primary, but this, he thought, was *Air* rather than Water.

This choice of Air as first principle enabled him to explain the origin of the other major elements in a much clearer and more matter of fact way than Anaximander. Propounding a new principle to explain all change, he maintained that Air is transformed into Fire by *rarefaction*, and into Water and Earth by *condensation*.

In its original condition Air, in his view, was of a uniform consistency and was invisible. It only became visible when its consistency was altered through 'thickening' or 'thinning'. Such alterations were, in effect, transformations of Air into the other elemental masses of Earth, Water, and Fire. Its transformations into these other elements were (and are) caused by an everlasting motion inherent in the nature of Air itself. This motion acted (and acts) to disperse or concentrate Air so that from time to time there is more or less of it in any given place. The formation of clouds followed by rain would have seemed to Anaximenes a clear instance of the process of *condensation* as a result of which water is produced from Air. Conversely, he would have noted the production of steam (= misty air) from boiling water as an example of *rarefaction*. When cooled, that is to say condensed, water obviously congealed into ice, and with that feeling for consistency already noted as characteristic of the Milesians, he went on to explain earth and rocks as the end products of still further condensations of Air. He compared the process to 'felting', a homely comparison based on observation of his city's woollen industry.

At the other end of the scale, he regarded Fire as an extremely 'relaxed' (his own term) or rarefied form of Air. *Qualities* like hot and cold were caused, in his view, by different *densities* of Air. He confirmed this point to his own satisfaction by the observation that air breathed out through an open mouth feels warm on the hand, but feels cold if blown out through compressed lips. Aristotle disputed this finding, arguing that two different masses of air were involved, the warm coming from inside us, and the cold originally outside us and pushed forward on to the hand by the blowing. But a faulty experiment does not invalidate Anaximenes's general contention. In effect, he was trying to explain differences of quality by differences of quantity, and this is rightly regarded as a seminal innovation in scientific thought.

Anaximenes's Air, like Anaximander's *apeiron*, was 'everlasting', so entitled to the epithet 'divine'. He probably conceived of Air, not as an inert material, but as the 'breath of life' sustaining the universe. This is to be inferred from the single complete sentence quoted from his work (which unfortunately contains some anachronistic terms and so must be more of a paraphrase than a verbatim quotation):

> Just as our soul, being air, holds our bodies together, breath-air encompasses the whole world.

The idea of a breath-soul is widespread and primitive. The originality of Anaximenes lay in taking up this primitive notion and giving it a cosmic application. Reflection on the connection between air, breath, and life was probably the stimulus to his adoption of Air as the primary principle. Air as a *vital* principle could plausibly be endowed with the power of movement, and through movement it could transform itself into the vast variety of things that make up our world. Anaximenes is even reported as deriving the gods of popular cult from the same airy source. It was a considerable intellectual achievement to account for every object, hot or cold, moist or dry, light or heavy, physical or psychic, by one very economical set of assumptions. Anaximenes is a worthy precursor of the long line of physicists whose dream has been to find one comprehensive formula to cover all the transformations of the physical universe.

GENERAL CONCLUSION

Why did these epoch-making intellectual advances first take place in Ionian Miletus rather than in one of the older civilisations of the Near East? Part of the answer must lie in the organisation of religion in Greek lands and its role in Greek life. Greece in general and Ionia in particular were remarkably free from priestly domination. In Babylonia and Egypt the priestly castes held a commanding position in the economy through the extensive estates attached to the temples. The priests also exercised great political power through their relationship with the monarchy. In Babylonia, for example, the king ruled of divine right, but his authority had to be annually confirmed by the high priest of Marduk. In both countries organised knowledge in medicine, mathematics, and astronomy was concentrated within the temple precincts, and so under priestly control. Intellectual enquiry was only possible within a received theological framework which buttressed the whole social order. By contrast, in Greek lands, the hand of religion rested much more lightly on society. The citizens respected the gods, but were not unduly subservient to them or their ministers. Temple cults lay on the fringes of political life, not at its centre. Industry and commerce were in the hands of laymen. Non-religious poetry flourished. Men were free to look for knowledge where they could find it, and free also to communicate their researches without the need to conform to a traditional theology.

Probable debts to Babylonian astronomy and Egyptian techniques of land-measurement have been mentioned above, and the great prosperity of Ionia was also a necessary precondition for the rise of independent speculation. But in the final analysis, the miracle of the birth of natural philosophy cannot be fully accounted for in terms of external influence or social conditions. The Ionian world seems to have been unusually well supplied with men of genius, and genius is to be revered not explained. In Miletus in the sixth century BC, three men of outstanding genius applied their creative talents to a new task, the task of giving a rational account of the world. They initiated scientific and philosophical enquiry by directing their relatively unprejudiced minds to the understanding of Nature as they observed it, freeing themselves as far as possible from presuppositions derived from traditional mythology. The result was a series of inspired generalisations about the origin and nature of the material universe, with special reference to the processes of natural change. From our superior standpoint we can see the factual errors in many of their detailed statements, but nothing can detract from the merit of the initiative they took, and it is not possible to overestimate the importance of the new spirit they brought into intellectual enquiry.

2

PYTHAGORAS AND PHILOSOPHY AS A WAY OF LIFE

PYTHAGORAS IS THE most famous name in Presocratic philosophy, but source problems have tended to obscure his reputation. The uncertainties of the record are taken so seriously by recent historians that they have become chary of attributing any philosophical originality at all to him, but this, I think, takes scepticism too far. A dominating personality lies behind the legend, and I believe that there was a remarkable mind there too.

The first problem is that not a single word survives from his pen, and it is not even certain whether he wrote anything — the ancients, like the moderns, were divided on this point. The second problem is that a veil of secrecy shrouded the brotherhood which he founded, especially at the outset. This means that one has to conjecture what doctrines, if any, he communicated to its original members. However, I think that it is possible to do this in a reasonably controlled way on the basis of some early and significant references made to him by contemporaries or near-contemporaries. The third problem relates to the dating and attribution of scientific discoveries within the Pythagorean Order, and is compounded by the pious tendency of its adherents to refer later discoveries in mathematics and astronomy back to the founder. The fourth problem stems from the hagiographical elements in the tradition which tend to obscure and down-grade Pythagoras as a thinker.

The Pythagorean system that emerges from the totality of all our sources is a strange blend of religious dogma and mathematical speculation. Much of the religious element is archaic, and its original formulation probably owed much to Pythagoras himself. The nub of the problem is to assess which (if any) elements on the scientific side go back to the founder, and which were due to later members. But first let me give an outline of Pythagoras's life, which is reasonably well documented, and which forms a credible and coherent whole.   .

Life of Pythagoras

Pythagoras was a native of the island of Samos. That much is certain, and the fact is significant. He was born *c*.570 and lived for the first half of his life in what was then one of the most powerful and progressive city-states of the Ionian League. In the sixth century Samian artists and engineers were famous for their ingenuity and bold inventiveness, and it was a technologically advanced society that nurtured his genius.

Samos lies quite close to Miletus, and Pythagoras must have been aware of the new developments in Milesian cosmology. His curiosity may well have taken him to hear Anaximander or Anaximenes. The Ephesian philosopher Heraclitus says that he was assiduous in enquiry, and that he 'excerpted the treatises', which at this period must mean the latest Ionian prose writings.

This Samos-based period of research came to an end because of his antipathy to the regime of the tyrant Polycrates, a highly successful and totally unscrupulous buccaneer who seized power in the island about 538. Pythagoras seems to have put up with his rule for some years before deciding to go into voluntary exile. He is said to have been about forty years of age when he emigrated to Croton in the south of Italy. This decisive move is to be dated *c*.530.

Croton was already famous for its athletes and doctors, and its noted physician Democedes, who had visited Samos, may have recommended it as a suitable place to settle. Pythagoras soon made a great impact on his adopted city, reviving its morale after a defeat by neighbouring Locri, and impressing young and old alike by his knowledge and eloquence. He was entrusted with the task of framing a new constitution, which was judged to be 'aristocratic' in the true sense because it ensured 'government by the best'. Before very long Pythagoras and his followers were in complete political control, having instituted the ancient equivalent of a 'rule of the saints'.

The changed circumstances of Croton are interestingly documented in its first issue of a silver coinage which dates from this period. The coins are very beautiful in design, and of a most unusual incuse type, and the issue may with considerable probability be attributed to the initiative of Pythagoras, whose father was a skilled engraver of gems.

But Pythagoras brought much more to Croton than Ionian political expertise and Samian artistry. The Order which he founded there became the first focus of philosophy in the world of the western Greek colonies. Hitherto Ionia had been the sole centre of intellectual advance, but now a gifted Ionian emigré had arrived to plant the seeds of philosophy in the fertile soil of Greek Italy. This philosophy aimed to provide its adherents with a rule of life as well as an explanation of the world. Its influence spread rapidly to other cities in the area, where 'cells' of Pythagoreans were soon established, and the Order continued to prosper long after Pythagoras's death, which occurred *c.*495.

Origins and character of the Pythagorean way of life

A distinctively *Greek* way of life, which marked out Hellene from 'barbarian', had already taken firm shape by the time Pythagoras was born. At the heart of this Greek way was the deliberate schooling of boys and young men in 'music' and 'gymnastics'. The Greeks were the first nation to make physical exercise a serious and systematic part of education, and the culture of the 'gymnasium' is one of their major legacies to mankind. Apart from its general influence in Greek life, athletics also played an important part in stimulating the development of a more scientific form of medicine. The 'know-how' of trainers and coaches in such matters as diet, massage, and the treatment of sprains and dislocations was fruitfully assimilated by the doctors of the time. The other twin pillar of this early Greek education was 'music', by which was meant a practical training in playing stringed instruments and in solo and choral singing. By the time he left school every Greek youth (of the upper classes at least) could strum a tune on the lyre, and had memorised much poetry embodying the religious and cultural traditions of his people.

Pythagoras built on the key points of this system, using it as a foundation on which to erect his more advanced and 'philosophic' kind of education for selected adults. In the words of a good ancient authority, his method involved 'medicine to purify the body and music to purify the soul'. In medical matters Pythagoras and his followers are said to have paid special attention to diet and the compatibility of various types of food and drink, and to have preferred external remedies such as poultices to drugs. They also developed a form of mental training which laid great stress on memory-building exercises such as the orderly recollection each morning of all that had been said or done on the previous day. Pythagoras was famous for his memory which, he claimed, even extended back to details of his previous incarnations. The whole system was 'ascetic' in the Greek sense, the word being derived from the systematic training (*askesis**) practised by athletes.

Pythagoras's lasting influence must, one feels, have derived from inspiring qualities as a teacher. Having worked out a disciplined rule of life for himself, he gathered a band of disciples round him and inspired them to emulate his example. Plato says that he was 'greatly loved' as an educator by his associates. Friendship and a sense of community were actively cultivated by religious injunctions and by instruction that aimed to give the members a real insight into the concordant nature of the universe. They were taught that the world, like human society, was held together by the orderly arrangement of its parts, and it then became their clear duty to cultivate order in their own lives.

In keeping with this new mode of instruction Pythagoras was said to have been the first to call himself a 'lover of wisdom' (*philosophos**), a more modest term than 'wise man' (*sophos**). He advocated the pursuit of knowledge rather than claiming its attainment. 'Philosophy' was a very suitable new term to characterise self-improvement and intellectual enquiry as a way of life.

The religious content of early Pythagoreanism
The Ionian philosopher-poet Xenophanes, who was an exact contemporary of Pythagoras, must have met and known many Pythagoreans in the course of his travels in western Greece. In one of his elegiac poems he gives an amusing and somewhat satirical portrait of Pythagoras in the following terms:

> He was once passing by when a man was beating a dog, and they say that he took pity on the animal and said: 'Stop beating it. Indeed it is the soul of a friend of mine. I recognised it when I heard its voice.'

This is perhaps the earliest reference to Pythagoras, and under the sarcasm it contains the valuable information, which is abundantly confirmed by later testimony, that Pythagoras believed in the transmigration of human souls into animal bodies.

The doctrine of transmigration (also called 'reincarnation' and 'metempsychosis') here makes its first appearance in extant Greek literature. A number of important consequences flow from this belief. First, it is a picturesque way of emphasising the essential unity and kinship of all forms of life, a central tenet for Pythagoreanism. Secondly, it has important implications for conduct, notably the ban on killing and eating animals. Thirdly, it follows that the soul survives the death of the body, and Pythagoras was certainly a firm believer in its immortality in a much more positive sense than was pictured in the shadowy survival of the 'souls' (=ghosts) in Homer. And, finally, the anecdote suggests that the lowly status of his friend's reincarnation in canine form was a punishment for shortcomings in his previous life.

All this may reasonably be taken to have formed part of Pythagoras's teaching. And we may go on to infer that he emphasised the need for amendment of life if a down-grading into animal shape was to be avoided. This is where the Pythagorean notion of purification comes strongly in. The doctrine of reincarnation implies a sharp division between soul and body, with the body regarded as no more than an impure and temporary container for a being with an immortal destiny. The ultimate aim of human conduct can then be represented as the purification of the soul by abstinence from bodily pleasures and by the contemplation of heavenly realities. The motto of the Pythagorean way of life was 'Follow God'. By these means the soul would win release from the 'wheel of becoming' and realise its true divine status. Anyone familiar with Indian thought will see many similarities, and it is a striking fact that Pythagoras and Siddartha Gautama, the Buddha, appear to have been almost exact contemporaries. But the possibility of any cross-currents of influence from one system to the other seems most remote.

There is much evidence that the Pythagoreans were required to abstain from meat. Their lives were also enlightened, and circumscribed, by a peculiar set of pithy sayings, known as 'things heard' (*akousmata**). Presumably the disciples originally heard these sayings from their 'guru' Pythagoras, and then assimilated and practised them out of respect for his superior status and wisdom.

It is not an unreasonable supposition that piety and science cohered in the character of Pythagoras himself. After all, Sir Isaac Newton devoted much time and effort to biblical chronology. Pythagoras's influence and his successful claim to superior status must ultimately, I think, have rested on the possession of really superior talents and insights. The legends that came to cluster about him indicate at the least a talent for showmanship, but this is not inconsistent with genuine ability. It is easy to be cynical about him, as Heraclitus was, and to dismiss him as a charlatan. But even Heraclitus admits that he had 'much learning', and the great fifth-century historian Herodotus called him 'not the weakest of the sages'. One has to take seriously the possibility that as well as being a religious and educational innovator, he may also have been a mathematical genius.

The discovery about the musical scale attributed to Pythagoras
Mention has been made of the central position of the lyre in early Greek education. This was a seven-stringed instrument in which four of the strings were tuned to fixed intervals. The two outermost strings were called 'high' and 'low' and spanned an *octave*. The 'middle' string was tuned to a *fourth* above the lowest (and hence to a *fifth* below the highest). The one next to it was tuned one tone higher (so it too stood in a *fourth/fifth* relationship to the outermost strings). The tuning of the remaining three strings varied according to the type of scale desired. Thus Greek music was grounded in three primary intervals, which the Greeks called 'concordant'.

Pythagoras was credited with the remarkable discovery that this basic melodic framework could be expressed in simple numerical terms, using the first four integers. The octave was represented by the ratio 1:2, the fifth by 2:3, the fourth by 3:4. These ratios basically compare the rates of vibration of the two strings responsible for the interval in question. It is not, however, certain whether Pythagoras knew this, and, even if he did, he could not have measured the rates by comparing weights or tensions as some later sources said he did. How then did he arrive at the discovery? He probably experimented with the *kanon*, a one-stringed instrument with a movable bridge (which tradition says he invented). Given that the tension of the string is constant, different notes are produced by stopping it at different intervals, and it is easy to see by experiment that if the sounding string is stopped at half its length and then plucked again it gives out a note an octave higher. The fifth (in the higher octave) can be produced by stopping down the string to a third of its length, the fourth by stopping it down to a quarter. Like many great discoveries it was in its way very simple, and

Pythagoras with his lively mind and skilled hands may well have been the one who made it.

The discovery is very satisfying to the human mind. It has the beautiful clarity and simplicity of the law of gravity or the periodic table of the elements. It encourages belief that the world is fundamentally a *kosmos**, an orderly place whose structure can be mastered by human intelligence. The doxographical tradition held that Pythagoras was the first to use the term 'cosmos' of the world as a whole, and it would not be surprising if he was encouraged to do so by his harmonic discoveries. Given the link between Greek musical education and early Pythagoreanism it is easy to see how his researches acquired epoch-making importance for the new school. The musicians went on tuning their instruments by ear, but now Pythagoras was able to explain the whole basis of their art in a simple mathematical way. They had the knack, but he *understood* what they were doing. They appreciated the quality of the sounds, but he *knew* the quantitative ratios on which they were based. This gave him a higher philosophical insight into what he doubtless regarded as the true nature of musical sounds. They could reasonably be viewed as the orderly outcome of imposing the *limiting* factor of number on the *unlimited* (and therefore disorderly) continuum of the vibrating string.

The Pythagorean development of mathematics

Aristotle's summary in the first book of his *Metaphysics* is the primary source. The tenets are attributed generally to 'those who are called Pythagoreans', and probably represent an amalgam of doctrines over several generations within the Order.

His first point is that the Pythagoreans were the first to advance the study of mathematics. He says that 'being schooled in such studies they considered that the principles of mathematics were the principles of all things'. This attitude may well have originated with Pythagoras and his first followers, since it is easy to imagine the discovery in harmonics being viewed as a golden key that could unlock the secrets of the whole of nature. The arithmetical formulation of the main musical intervals was as fundamental in its way as the discovery that water is H_2O.

Flushed by their progress in mathematics the Pythagoreans, Aristotle continues, jumped to the grand conclusion that 'the elements of number are the elements of all things'. By 'elements of number' they meant 'odd' and 'even', since all integers are either odd or even, and they equated oddness with 'limit' and evenness with 'the unlimited'. For some members of the school these two principles of Limit (Oddness) and the Unlimited (Evenness) were a sufficient starting-point for the explanation, and indeed the generation, of the whole universe.

Pythagoras's theorem

The Pythagoreans used to represent numbers in spatial form by dots arranged in regular patterns (as we still do on dice or dominoes). Various series of odd and even numbers were given triangular, oblong, and square shape (hence the origin of the term 'square root'). Given that Pythagoras knew of the advances in geometry attributed to Thales (see p.19), further investigation of the properties of 'triangular' and 'square' numbers could have led him to formulate and prove the famous theorem about the square on the hypotenuse of a right-angled triangle which tradition assigns to his name. That this square equals the sum of the squares on the other two sides is of course true of all right-angled triangles, but a special perfection attached to the triangle the length of whose sides was in the proportion 3:4:5. Given three lines of these lengths the resulting triangle has to be right-angled, and this fact had long been known and used by land-surveyors in Egypt. Progressive decipherment of Babylonian cuneiform has also shown that the theorem was known to Chaldean mathematicians many centuries before Pythagoras. It is no longer possible to assert that it was an 'original' discovery of his, but he might have proved it in a new way by integrating it into the structure of his arithmetical geometry.

Pythagorean astronomy

The mathematical and *a priori* character of Pythagorean thinking seems to have had a liberating effect on their minds, fostering a bold and imaginative approach to astronomical problems. In some sources Pythagoras is said to have been the first to assert that the earth is a sphere. Later members of the School broke away, not merely from the flat earth theories of the Ionians, but from the view that the earth forms the unmoving centre of the cosmos. Hicetas of Syracuse (perhaps *fl. c.*500) suggested that the earth was revolving rapidly on its own axis, thus producing the illusion of movement in the heavenly bodies. An even bolder hypothesis was produced by other members of the school. This theory displaced our planet from the centre of the universe, and maintained that it in company with the sun and the other heavenly bodies circled round a 'central fire'.

These speculations about the earth's movement were never generally accepted in the ancient world, but they were not totally forgotten either, and a record of them was known to Copernicus. He refers to them in the preface to his epoch-making work on the revolutions of the heavenly bodies, and says that they gave him courage to pursue the hypothesis 'although it seemed absurd' that the earth itself was in motion. There could hardly be a more effective tribute to the lasting influence of Pythagoras and his School.

Conclusion
In contrast to the Milesian preoccupation with material elements the Pythagoreans emphasised *form* as the crucial factor in the constitution of things. They also revered mathematics as the key to knowledge. Both these points were seminal and central in the later development of Platonic metaphysics, and Plato was also the spiritual heir to Pythagoras in his doctrine of the soul, and in his exaltation of philosophy to a centrally important position in human life and politics.

3

HERACLITUS, PROPHET AND SAGE

HERACLITUS WAS BORN and lived out his life in the rich commercial city-state of Ephesus. His prime was anciently put in the sixty-ninth Olympiad (504–1), which implies a life-span of from c.540 to c.480. This dating is consistent with his polemical attacks on Pythagoras and Xenophanes, who were active in the second half of the sixth century. From 546 on Ephesus formed part of the Persian Empire, so Heraclitus, the least subservient of philosophers, lived and died a Persian subject.

A note of arrogance permeates his writing, no doubt deriving as much from his aristocratic lineage as from his intellectual superiority. He was descended from the royal founder of Ephesus, and held an hereditary 'kingship', which in practice would have meant responsibility for priestly duties, but these he resigned to his brother. It was not in his nature to be conformist in religious practice, and he remarked that 'praying to a statue is like chatting to your house'.

Heraclitus was no democrat. His saying 'Lawlessness should be quenched quicker than a fire' has a good lordly ring to it. But he was no tyrant either. Some of his most memorable sayings relate to the importance of the rule of law. He believed that all human laws were 'nourished' by one divine law, and that in consequence 'the people should defend their laws like their city-wall'.

He is certainly to be credited with at least one 'book' which he is said to have deposited in the temple of Ephesian Artemis. The 'book' may have been more of a collection of aphorisms than a continuous treatise. There are indications that it was always a rarity, and at first there may have been only one copy of it. In those early days of philosophy books were far from readily available. There were no publishing firms, no book-shops, no libraries. Heraclitus tells us that he listened to the lectures of others, and he probably preferred to communicate his own philosophy orally. The dedication in the temple may have been designed to underline the inspirational quality of his message.

The surviving corpus of his work comprises some 125 fragments, give or take a few whose genuineness in whole or part is disputed. Most of them are short, pungent, and memorable, and not a few of them are distinctly obscure. The obscurity was to some extent deliberate. Heraclitus was anciently dubbed 'The Riddler', and it is clear that he liked riddles and thought them a suitable device for conveying the paradoxical nature of the truth of things. But it is possible to over-emphasise his obscurity. In general, I think, he tends to express himself in a pregnant or allusive, rather than obscure, way. The power and artistry of his style are notable, and he is often and rightly called 'oracular'.

Discussion of Heraclitus's style shades easily into exposition of his thought. His allusive manner is related to his belief that truth is hidden rather than obvious. He wanted to reveal the true nature of the world, but, as he said, 'nature loves to hide herself'. Hence his frequent recourse to homely analogies designed, like parables, to help his hearers to penetrate to the hidden recesses of reality. It is a commonplace to call him a prophet, and we may compare his command, 'Listen not to me [as a person] but to what I say', with the Old Testament formula, 'Hear the word of the Lord'.

The source of his inspiration was his own understanding. 'I went looking for myself' is one of the most revealing of the fragments. It marks his method as being very different from that of the Milesians, who looked outwards in search of nature. Heraclitus looked into his own mind, and seems to have found the clue to the riddle of the universe in the hidden depths and complexities of the human psyche (*psuche**).

The *logos* of Heraclitus

At the outset of his book he contrasts the truth of his message with the inability of most people to comprehend it. The opening sentences run as follows:

> This my account is a true account and always will be, but men
> are always incapable of understanding it, both before they

41

hear it and when first they have heard it. All things happen in accordance with this account, but men seem like untried novices when they make trial of such words and facts as I expound, as I determine each thing according to [its] nature and declare how it is.

The Greek for 'account' is *logos**, a Protean word which later came to acquire more specialised meanings such as a 'general principle' (in philosophy), 'proportion' (in mathematics), and 'Divine Reason' (in theology). One risks anachronism by importing such meanings into the present passage, and in my translation I have kept to the basic meaning of the word in the ordinary Greek of the time, namely, 'statement', or 'account'.

The *logos* is what Heraclitus has to say, but it is not just a personal statement (which would be open to his condemnation of private opinion), but a considered and objective account of the nature of things, the 'real story', as we say in English. It has explanatory value, as the second sentence makes clear. Heraclitus is confident that his account will be accepted once it is understood. He says elsewhere that 'thought is common to all', and he insists that intelligent discourse, as a reflection of thought, is also common to all, and should prove as acceptable to all rational beings as common law to the community.

So much for the beginning of the book. I proceed next to consider the paradox which has been generally thought to embody his central philosophical insight, the doctrine of the identity of 'opposites'.

The doctrine of opposites

Heraclitus rejected the ultimate validity of distinctions such as day/night, winter/summer, up/down, war/peace, life/death. These and other so-called 'opposites' must, he thought, be viewed together since neither can exist without the other. Their co-existence as part of the same continuum is the fundamental truth about them. Each pair is basically one, not two, and each term becomes meaningful only in the light of the other. 'It is disease that makes health sweet and good...' Part of his meaning is that the difference between 'opposites' is relative to the experiencing subject, as in the case of sea-water which is 'safe and drinkable to fish, but undrinkable and destructive to men'. He also insists that sea-water really is simultaneously 'most pure and most foul'. Aristotle quotes an important general statement of this theme which, it has been suggested, may have stood as the conclusion of the whole book: 'Conjunctions [are] wholes and not-wholes, convergently drawing apart, harmoniously discordant, one from all and all from one.'

The dark sayings just quoted are rendered somewhat more luminous by two other important fragments. The first contains his famous comparison of reality with a bow or a lyre:

> They do not comprehend how in drawing apart it comes to agree with itself. Harmony [is] backward-turning like that of bow and lyre.

Bow and lyre are complex objects whose stability and efficiency depend on the maintenance of the opposed tensions set up between strings and frame. If a string snaps one becomes all too well aware of these hidden but all-important tensions.

The second fragment reads:

> Hidden structure is stronger than visible structure.

In this second fragment the word translated 'structure' (*harmonia**) is the same as that translated 'harmony' in the first. It conveys the notion that any worthwhile structure, whether in society or the world of nature, is the product of a conflict which has been so adjusted that opposite forces are made to co-exist simultaneously in a state of reciprocal tension.

The tension of opposites and world process
Heraclitus seems to have conceived of world process in terms of the action and reaction of mutually opposed movements. The process was powered by forces whose hidden tensions balance out to produce an '*ordered* world'. He expressed this conception in the striking phrase: 'Thunder-bolt steers the universe.' The metaphor of 'steering' is a dynamic image designed to evoke the idea of pressure and counter-pressure familiar to sailors when the hand on the tiller works constantly to counteract the forces of wind and wave. Heraclitus also makes use of the overtones of the 'thunder-bolt', Zeus's supreme weapon, to express his conception of the awesome and dominating power that keeps the material world on course. This power is always at work below the apparently stable surface of

43

things (like atomic energy), and manifests itself from time to time in the terrifying phenomena of the thunder-storm.

Heraclitus did not think that the world had been created by this fiery force, for in his view the world had no beginning and would have no end. His rejection of any cosmogony is expressed as follows:

> The order [*kosmos*], which is the same for all, no god nor man has made it, but it always existed, does exist, and will exist: ever-living fire, being kindled in measures and being quenched in measures.

This majestic utterance is rich with meaning. In speaking of the ever-living fire which is kindled and quenched 'in measures' Heraclitus is bidding us view the cosmos as an orderly dynamic *process* rather than a miscellaneous collection of static masses. Like his Milesian predecessors he recognised the existence of the great expanses of Air, Water, and Earth, but did not assign primary importance to them. The fundamental reality for him was either Fire, or something best represented by Fire. The fire that became visible in the heavenly bodies was for him a manifestation of the invisible, restless, fiery energy underpinning the whole cosmic process.

There were two major movements in this process, here called 'kindling' and 'quenching', but elsewhere described as the 'way up' and the 'way down'. It is no surprise to find him telling us that 'the way up and the way down are one and the same'. Two people may travel simultaneously in different directions between two towns but they use the same road, and in this sense there is a permanent way which is the same for both. This is the concept conveyed by his description of the cosmic Fire as 'ever-living', and also as being 'kindled and quenched'. I follow the view that the blazing up and the dying down of Fire are to be thought of as going on continually and simultaneously. The kindling is the 'way up' to incandescent vapour, the quenching the 'way down' to dampness and solidity. Heraclitus refers to the process as the 'turnings of Fire', that is, the transformations by which Fire is condensed downwards into sea and earth and simultaneously (though some would maintain 'later') exhaled upwards to become Fire again.

The details of this process are obscure in our sources, but the general outline is clear enough. All physical change is being viewed as a two-way, self-perpetuating process. The process is fathered by Strife, but Heraclitus also lays great stress on its ordered nature, using the notion of 'measures', a term that constantly turns up in the fragments that bear on movement and change. The measures are prescribed by cosmic 'justice', a universal law of nature ordaining reasonable norms for the co-functioning of 'opposites'.

In a key fragment Heraclitus pictures the world process as a continuous two-way exchange between Fire and all other perceived objects:

> All things are an exchange for Fire, and Fire for all things, like goods for gold and gold for goods.

The comparison, as always, is effective, and gains added piquancy from the fact that the earliest extant Greek coins (*c.*600BC) were recovered from a foundation deposit in the archaic temple of Artemis at Ephesus. One hundred years later the great Ephesian philosopher is using the idea of monetary transaction, in which his city had been a pioneer, to point up his concept of a 'fire-standard' in terms of which all physical transformations can be evaluated. When Fire is quenched to form Sea there must be an equivalent in the new 'opposite' which will enable it to be cashed in again for Fire. The measure of Fire is the common measure of all things, analogous to the old mercantile concept of a 'gold-standard'.

The doctrine of flux

Plato attributes to Heraclitus the dictum that 'all things move and nothing remains still', and adds that he compared reality to the flow of a river, saying that 'one could not step twice into the same river'. This is often referred to as the doctrine of Universal Flux. It has been argued that Plato is paraphrasing rather than quoting, that he is attributing to Heraclitus the developed views of one of his later followers called Cratylus, and that 'universal flux' is not to be found in the thought of the master himself. If 'universal flux' implies random disorderly motion in the heart of things and a world that is chaotic rather than cosmic, then it is certainly not the doctrine of Heraclitus. But if the phrase implies only a constant and orderly transformation of one thing into another, then we may with good reason attribute it to him. Even the most sceptical of modern commentators accept that he did say: 'Other and other waters flow down on those who step into the same rivers.' The point must surely be that rivers, like bows and lyres, exemplify the co-existence of 'opposites', in this case 'sameness' and 'difference'. We talk about the 'same' river because it is a relatively permanent feature of the landscape, with its direction and flow controlled, as we would say, by the law of gravity. But when we mentally analyse the contents of the river we must agree that it never consists of the same portion of water in the same place. A river is an excellent symbol for the measured and continuous change that constitutes the essence of the Heraclitean universe.

Intelligent control in the cosmos

Heraclitus considered that the warfare and tension between 'opposites' is a good thing because it is the only way in which the equilibrium of the world can be maintained. 'It is necessary,' he said, 'to realise that war is common to all, and justice strife, and that all things happen in accordance with strife and necessity.' Anaximander branded the warfare of the Opposites as an encroachment and an injustice. Heraclitus commends it as the true justice. This is the stern and, some would say, brutal conclusion of his cosmic analysis. It explains his criticism of Homer's prayer that Strife might disappear from among gods and men. It explains his antipathy to Pythagoras who listened for the 'harmony of the spheres'. But Heraclitus is not preaching mindless anarchy. On the contrary he regards his Law of Strife as a manifestation of divine intelligence and justice.

'Human character', he proclaimed, 'lacks intelligent judgement, but the divine possesses it.' Another fragment (whose text is not quite certain) seems to picture the 'intelligent judgement' which 'steers all things through all things'. Since a previously quoted fragment (p.43) describes this steering as done by the thunder-bolt, it is reasonable to conclude that for Heraclitus the intelligent ordering of all things stemmed from the primacy of Fire. The cosmic Fire is 'ever-living', and so to the Greek mind 'divine'. It is the 'hand on the tiller' of the world, operating not from outside the world, but within and through it.

Soul and world process

One ancient critic held that the work of Heraclitus was political rather than philosophic in intent. He called it 'accurate steering towards the goal of life'. There is something to be said for this interpretation. One important political aspect has already been touched on, namely its stress on law as the common and rational factor in the ordering of communities. The system also has novel psychological and ethical dimensions.

It is clear that the philosopher who 'went looking for himself' must have thought long and hard about the nature of 'soul'. That he found it an important but baffling subject is indicated by the saying: 'You could never discover the limits of soul though you travelled over every road; it has such a deep *logos*.' As mentioned above, *logos* in Heraclitus is an account that explains the nature of a thing. The reference to travelling 'every road' suggests observation and enquiry, while 'deep' suggests that there is a hidden, or spiritual, dimension to 'soul' which calls for a different, perhaps more intuitive, approach to its mysteries.

It is not altogether surprising, then, to find that the extant fragments do little more than hint at the nature and destiny of 'soul'. Heraclitus seems to have conceived of animate life flowing swiftly through the limbs of the organism like a moist stream, with the conscious soul exhaled from it just as fiery vapours are exhaled from the sea. Soul would then have a natural tendency to follow the 'upward path' to the Fiery Intelligence which is 'only-wise', and it would be the duty of an intelligent person to enhance this tendency by appropriate conduct. The nature of such conduct is indicated by his condemnation of drunkenness, and his remark that 'dry soul is wisest and best'. The downward path into the moist basis of life was to be avoided, for 'it is death to souls to become water'. The upward path called for self-discipline and the avoidance of excessive pleasure.

Wise living for him, then, would seem to have been a form of communion through the intellect with the objective processes of the real world, and would have demanded a total dedication to the 'upward path'. Only by these means could one win release from the private and particular illusions in which most people remain imprisoned. By this standard the popular mystery cults, involving drunken and frenzied identification with Dionysus through group hysteria, would remain a grotesque and unholy parody of genuine philosophical initiation, and it is small wonder that he roundly condemned such religious practices.

Conclusion

Despite the curt and enigmatic character of the fragments a remarkably coherent view of the world emerges, with a strong emphasis on law-governed process at the heart of all physical transformations. The Heraclitean system continued to attract disciples down to Plato's day, and one of them, the Athenian Cratylus, had a decisive, if negative, influence on the development of Plato's thought about the physical world and man's perception of it. The early Stoics were whole-hearted admirers of him, and incorporated what one might call his 'theology' of Fiery Wisdom into their own dogmatic worldview. They also took up and expanded his embryonic notion of the 'natural' basis of human law. Another seminal aspect of Heraclitus lay in his appreciation of the effect that philosophical understanding could and should have on human conduct. He shared this insight with Pythagoras and his followers, helping to develop the conception of 'philosophy' as a 'way of life', and thus advancing the subject beyond the ethically neutral speculations of the Milesians.

4

PHILOSOPHICAL ARGUMENT BEGINS AT ELEA

ELEA WAS A Greek colony in southern Italy whose foundation, *c*.540, by refugees from Ionian Phocaea came as a direct result of the advance of Persia to the Aegean a few years before. The enforced migration of the Phocaeans helped to spread the seed of Ionian speculation to the western Greek world of Italy and Sicily where Greek city-states had already been in existence for upwards of 150 years. Elea provided a temporary resting place for the philosopher-poet Xenophanes, himself a refugee from Ionian Colophon. It is quite possible that he joined in the original colonisation. He certainly took an interest in the place and wrote a poem on its history in 2000 lines (not extant) which presumably celebrated the exploits of the bold Phocaeans.

Elea soon became a noted centre for philosophy, as it was the birth-place and home of the great Parmenides and his famous pupil Zeno. The ancient historians of philosophy regarded Xenophanes too as a member of the Eleatic School, and the 'succession' writers claimed that he was the teacher of Parmenides, but there is no other evidence of this, and the connection between their thought is quite peripheral.

Xenophanes (*c*.570–480) is chiefly significant for his criticisms of Greek polytheism, and for his highly original speculations about the nature of deity. He propounded a refined and enlightened monotheism, and has a good claim to be regarded as the founder of natural theology. His extant fragments total over one hundred lines; the longer pieces run to description or satire rather than philosophy, but enough survives from his poem *On Nature* to justify his place among the innovative thinkers of the period.

49

PARMENIDES

Life and writings

Parmenides is the key figure in the development of Presocratic thought. He is also the first philosopher whose writings survive (in part at least) in a reasonably full and coherent form. In his thought the critical spirit of early Ionia blossomed in a new and radical way, gaining, it seems, fresh vigour from its transplanting to western Greek soil.

A native of the young colony of Elea, he was born about 514, and his family is said to have been wealthy and aristocratic. The main formative influence on his thought came from his contacts with the Pythagorean Order. He was a close associate of a Pythagorean called Ameinias, and dedicated a shrine to his memory. Such an action would not be inconsistent with the complexities of character that seem to be reflected in his work. He exhibits an unusual blend of mystical fervour and hard-headed rationalism, at one moment proclaiming his message with prophetic zeal, and at the next supporting it with profound and penetrating arguments that decisively altered the course of Greek philosophy.

Parmenides chose to publish his views in hexameter verse with a strong Homeric colouring. This was a deliberate departure from the prose tradition established by the Milesians. Just as Homer sang at the prompting of the Muses, so Parmenides claimed divine inspiration, casting his work in the form of a revelation from a goddess. After an elaborate prelude (thirty-two lines, all extant), the poem fell into two distinct parts, now generally referred to as 'The Way of Truth' and 'The Way of Opinion (or Seeming)'. We have about eighty lines (most) of 'The Way of Truth', but only approximately thirty lines of 'The Way of Opinion'. Fortunately the better-preserved part is the more important, and I shall concentrate on that. The contents of the second part were never as significant or as influential.

Thought: 'The Way of Truth'

The first part of the poem presents an uncompromisingly monistic view of the world. In the light of pure reason Parmenides affirms the absolute unity and permanence of the One. He seems to have had a philosophic intuition of the ultimate nature of reality not unlike the vision of the poet Vaughan, who wrote:

50

I saw Eternity the other night
Like a great ring of pure and endless light,
   All calm as it was bright...

Vaughan goes on to describe time moving like a dark shadow below eternity, and carrying our world along with it. Parmenides, however, does not tolerate the existence of any world on a lower level than that of pure unchanging reality. He draws his contrasts very sharply and starkly. 'What is, is; what is not, is not.' The total completeness of reality prevents it entering into any other state than that in which it presently is. Time is thus excluded from the real world, and so too are motion and change. This is his revelation of the truth of things, and he argues that it is confirmed by the verdict of reason. His conclusions were totally at odds with all previous Ionian speculation, which set out to explain change, not to abolish it.

In Parmenides's view one cannot appeal to the senses in this matter, for the senses are completely untrustworthy. If they indicate a world of objects in change or motion that is a measure of their deceitfulness. Through the senses illusory opinions are imposed upon the mind. The philosopher must not put any trust in the apparent evidence of his senses. 'The Way of Opinion' is always a way of deception. This absolute rejection of sense-perception as a valid basis for knowledge initiated a great epistemological debate about appearance and reality which ran on down through all later Greek speculation.

The surviving extracts from 'The Way of Truth' represent the earliest piece of continuous philosophical argument to survive in the European tradition. Here is the passage which follows immediately after the prelude:

Come now, I shall speak, and you must hear and receive my word. These are the only roads of enquiry that exist for the thinking mind: one road, that 'IT IS', and that 'IT CANNOT NOT BE' is the path of Persuasion, for Truth attends it. Another road, that 'IT IS NOT', and that 'IT [i.e. what is not] MUST BE NON-EXISTENT' is a road that I declare to be totally indiscernible. For you could neither know [or recognise?] what is non-existent, for that is unattainable, nor could you describe it. For it is the same thing which is for thinking and for being.

51

In this difficult, but crucial, passage the expression is strained at times, but also monumentally impressive. Parmenides here recognises the existence of two possible roads of intellectual enquiry.

Road (A) consists of two basic propositions that must be accepted if the thinker is to proceed to grasp reality: IT IS and IT·CANNOT NOT BE. If told that 'it is', one's natural reaction is to ask 'What is?' Here this amounts to asking: 'What (if anything) does Parmenides have in mind as the subject of his basic statement IT IS? (The Greek for 'it is' is *esti*, and I follow those who take the word in an existential sense, rather than in the predicative sense which it can also have in Greek. There is the same ambiguity in English 'is'. Compare 'God is', meaning 'God exists', with 'God is good'.) There is no consensus as to how this question should be answered. I shall merely say that I favour the solution that finds the answer in the last sentence of the extract: 'it is the same thing which is for thinking and for being.' This is sometimes translated: 'Thought and Being are one and the same', a crisper rendering that gives the gist of Parmenides's position, provided one accepts that Thought is controlled by Being, and not *vice versa*. Parmenides is saying that one can validly think only about what really exists. On this basis, the subject of 'it is' will be 'whatever can be thought about, or enquired into'. His statement is the foundation charter of Rationalism, as fundamental in its way as Descartes's 'I think, therefore I am'.

Road (B), the way of Not-Being, is the prohibited way that enquiry must not follow, and indeed it seems self-evident that the 'non-existent' cannot be known nor recognised. We are inclined to agree that knowledge must relate to existent objects. Certainly it would be hard to recognise something that does not exist. We might however demur to the assertion that it is impossible to state or declare 'what is not'. What about the statement: 'The present King of France is not married'? Parmenides would give short shrift to such cavils. Your assertion, he would say, is not a philosophical statement. You are just playing with words. Remember my basic principle: 'The same thing is for thinking and for being.' Since the present King of France is not for being, that is, does not exist, he is not for thinking either. Parmenides is urging us to test our thinking by the touchstone of reality. The twin propositions: 'What is, is' and 'What is not, is not' are valuable signposts on the road to knowledge, clearing the mind of half-baked opinions.

52

There is a third Road (C) which is more popular than Road (B), and Parmenides is even more vehement in prohibiting its use. Those who travel it — and they include the majority of mankind — attempt to 'have it both ways' by asserting 'it is' together with 'it is not'. They will tell you, for example, that they have one body with many parts, thus asserting unity and plurality of the same object. They will say that their children share a family resemblance but have different temperaments, thus asserting likeness and unlikeness of the same group. Parmenides calls this road a 'backward-turning path', meaning that it is full of contradictions. The same adjective, 'backward-turning', also appears in a striking phrase of Heraclitus: 'backward-turning harmony' (see p.43). It has therefore been suggested that Parmenides is attacking Heraclitus for trading in contradictions, and it is indeed likely that he has him in mind. But Heraclitus is not his only target, merely a leading offender in the purveying of contradictions.

Parmenides wants to jolt people out of their customary view of things based on sense-perception and received opinion. He regards them as 'plying an unseeing eye and an echoing ear' and as using their tongues parrot-wise to repeat unthought-out sentiments. His positive injunction is to 'judge by argument' his 'much-contested refutation'. His refutation consists in the wholesale rejection of the concepts of change, motion, and becoming (*kinesis** and *genesis**), concepts which most people accept without thinking in the commerce of everyday life, but which, for Parmenides, are riddled with intolerable contradictions.

What does Parmenides put in their place? His answer may be summarised as follows. The true concept of reality excludes motion, change, and becoming. What truly exists has not come into existence, nor will it pass out of existence. It is both ungenerated and imperishable. It is complete, whole, motionless, and unending. Past and future tenses do not apply to it, 'since it is now, all of it together, one and continuous'. Parmenides affirms the reality of an All which is One. The concept of a thing 'coming into existence' implies that there was a previous time when it did not exist. But this concept lies on the forbidden road of not-being. Similarly the concept of 'destruction' implies that something will in the future pass out of existence. But this concept too lies on the forbidden road. Parmenides claims that his logic is just and binding. Anyone who wants to think correctly must avoid using terms that imply coming into, or passing out of, being. Motion is similarly excluded from Reality by the argument that the All has no imperfections and lacks nothing. Therefore it remains 'the same and in the same condition', and that which remains strictly in the same condition cannot move, for movement is a form of alteration, namely, alteration of position.

'The Way of Truth' ends with a very striking description of the All or the One as 'like the mass of a well-rounded sphere, equally balanced in every direction from centre to circumference'. Is this World Sphere a material or an immaterial object? The question would almost certainly have been meaningless for Parmenides, for no firm and philosophical distinction between the corporeal and the incorporeal had yet been drawn. Parmenides is asking us to *think* the Universe, rather than to attempt to imagine or perceive it. We tend to visualise the heavenly bodies as spheres moving through empty space. For Parmenides there is no empty space, since the All is a *plenum*, and no movement, since the All is at rest. So one should let his image of the motionless sphere expand in one's thought until it becomes equivalent to the sum total of all that is. In the geometry of Euclid straight lines can be indefinitely extended. For Einstein space is curved, and the universe finite but unbounded. Parmenides's sphere of reality seems Einsteinian rather than Euclidean. The comparison is his way of emphasising the perfection of reality, for the sphere is the perfect figure whose surface is one and continuous in all directions.

Conclusion

Parmenides's rational Monism was very different from the monistic approach of the Milesian School. They had posited a single primary stuff from which they derived the multiplicity of objects, and had sought to explain all change in terms of modification of this 'beginning'. Parmenides argued that there was no rational justification for positing any multiplicity or any change. They had trusted their senses to supply the basic data about the world. Parmenides rejected sense-perception as a road to truth. The system of Heraclitus which stressed the ultimate reality of Process was if anything even more opposed to the rigid view of Being propounded from Elea. Pythagoreanism was a dualistic system, so it too came under the ban of Parmenidean logic.

It was clear that rational thought about the world could make no progress until it found some way of refuting or by-passing the Parmenidean position. All subsequent thinkers down to Aristotle took account of his stringent logic, and all except Zeno suggested various ways in which his objections to multiplicity and change could be met. Zeno contented himself with developing new ways to refute Pluralism, and to him I now turn.

ZENO

Life and writings

Zeno, the arch-controversialist of antiquity, remains a very controversial figure. Some consider him a mere logic-chopper. For others his thought possesses great originality and depth. The view that he was attacking the basis of Pythagorean physics no longer finds as much support as it once did. Equally, the common view (based on Plato's account of him) that he was a staunch defender of Parmenidean Monism needs to be handled with considerable caution.

Very little is known about his life, and sadly little survives from his writings. Only four fragments are extant, amounting to no more than twenty-five lines in all, together with some brief summaries of other arguments. He is undoubtedly to be credited with one book of major significance which Plato calls a work of his youth. He may have written more in later life, but this is far from certain.

Plato summarises one of the arguments from the youthful work at the start of his dialogue *Parmenides*. In the same context we are also told that Zeno was some twenty-five years younger than Parmenides, that he was 'tall and of a pleasing appearance', and that he came on a visit to Athens in Parmenides's company. He must then have been born *c.*490, and he was certainly a native of Elea, but apart from this nothing significant is recorded about his career.

The youthful work is said to have contained forty 'arguments' or 'theses', and these were set out in a form new to philosophical writing. This novel style of argumentation led Aristotle to call him 'the discoverer of dialectic', by which he meant that Zeno pioneered the art of arguing from premises stated by other thinkers, or from premises commonly accepted. His object was to refute these premises by revealing latent contradictions.

Zeno's taste for controversy is abundantly illustrated in our sources. He does not emerge as a creative thinker, but rather as one who systematically attacked the views of others. He did this by a method of *hypothetical* argument, asking: 'If X is true, what follows?' And what follows, as he develops the argument, is always a set of propositions that contradict each other, with the result that the original hypothesis (*hupothesis**) is thereby shown to have been absurd.

His main intention, as represented by Plato, was to provide an indirect defence of Parmenidean Monism by demonstrating that those who ridiculed Parmenides for absurdities were themselves caught in even worse contradictions. This is usually taken to mean that he supported the Parmenidean hypothesis that All is One, but it is by no means clear that this is so. The evidence does not rule out his having regarded that hypothesis too as leading to contradictions.

Thought: paradoxes of plurality

Parmenides had affirmed the unity of Being, and denied the reality of motion. These affirmations run directly counter to the common-sense perception that the world contains a multiplicity of objects in motion. So Zeno took up the assumptions that 'things are many' and 'things move', and subjected them to a critical analysis which revealed unsuspected logical problems in the concepts of space, time, and extension.

Three of the four extant fragments come from the same extended passage of commentary by Simplicius. They revolve round the concept of the 'parts' of a (spatially extended) 'thing'. If these parts are really separate parts, they must, Zeno argues, constitute an *infinite plurality* of parts because each of them will be infinitely divisible. He then, in effect, formulates a dilemma by asking whether these parts themselves have a magnitude. If you say Yes, then Zeno points out that your 'thing' will be infinitely large. If you say No, he points out that your 'thing' will then have no size at all. It seems to follow that there cannot be a plurality of parts in anything.

Nor can a plurality of *things* be conceived without also generating contradictions. A short citation of Zeno's actual proof of this point will serve to give the flavour of his style and method:

(A) If things are many, they must be as many as they are, neither more nor less. And if they are as many as they are, they will be finite [namely, in quantity].

(B) If things are many, the things that exist are infinite. For there are always other things between the things that exist, and again others between those others, and so the things that exist are infinite [namely, in quantity].

The same hypothesis is neatly made to lead to directly opposed conclusions. The second horn of the dilemma (B) involves the assumption that for a thing to exist it must possess some extension in space. Simplicius has earlier given a separate Zenonian proof of this point. It will then be possible, in thought at least, to cut any thing in two, and each of the resultant parts can itself be bisected, and so on *ad infinitum*. An infinity of things is thereby generated, and this stands in contradiction to the finite number of things deduced in the first horn of the dilemma (A).

Paradoxes of motion
The argument based on bisection was known as 'the dichotomy', and appears to have been a favourite move with Zeno. It is prominent in the famous paradoxes against motion. We do not have these extant in Zeno's own words, but Aristotle gives a summary of four of them in his *Physics*.

The best known is 'Achilles and the tortoise'. The tortoise is pitted in a race against Achilles, and is given a head-start of a hundred units. By the time Achilles has covered this distance, the tortoise has moved on ten units. Achilles soon covers the ten units, but the tortoise is still one unit ahead. On the assumption that the intervening space is infinitely divisible, it seems to follow that Achilles will never overhaul the tortoise — at least not in a finite period of time.

Aristotle points out that the magnitudes in this argument are not divided in half, but that basically the same method of dichotomy *ad infinitum* is employed. His refutation is also succinct (though many hold it misses the point): 'It is false to claim that the one in front is not overtaken. It is not overtaken *so long as it is in front*. But yet it *is* overtaken (provided you grant that the runners can traverse a finite distance).'

A second paradox is 'The flying arrow'. At every moment in its flight the arrow occupies a space equal to its own length. But for a thing to occupy a space equal to itself is equivalent to its being at rest. Therefore the arrow is at rest in every moment of its flight.

Aristotle implies that Zeno's underlying assumption here is that time, like space, is infinitely divisible, consisting of an indefinite number of separate 'instants'. The flying arrow is, as it were, mentally photographed at rest in each of these instants. (This is a good example of how the intellect always tends to spatialise time.) But, says Aristotle, 'time is not composed of indivisible instants'.

The man of action will solve the puzzles by successfully racing a tortoise or shooting off an arrow. This may hit the target, but it will miss the point. The point is that Zeno raised difficult intellectual problems about the nature of space and time, and these must be tackled by intellectual methods as rigorous as his own. His arguments have been endlessly discussed ever since, but there is no agreed solution to the difficulties they raise. The crisp ingenuity of his paradoxes has ensured him immortality.

GENERAL CONCLUSION

The rise of the Eleatic School has now been outlined. At the heart of it lies the strictly argued Monism of Parmenides. Zeno, I think, was no more than an out-rider, a controversialist attacking pluralist views but not adding anything positive to the Parmenidean position. His importance lies in the impetus he gave to controlled argumentation as a way of making philosophical points. He was a pioneer in logic rather than metaphysics. Subsequent consideration of the arguments of Parmenides and Zeno led ultimately to the rise of Atomism, which will be described in Chapter 6. But first we must look at two gifted individuals, Empedocles and Anaxagoras, who developed their own very distinctive systems of thought in an attempt to rescue the Ionian world-picture from the conceptual difficulties raised by the Eleatics.

5

INDIVIDUAL SYSTEM-BUILDERS OF THE MID-FIFTH CENTURY

EMPEDOCLES

Life and writings

Empedocles of Acragas (c.492–432) stands out as one of the most colourful and flamboyant figures in the history of thought. Everything about him had star quality. His family was aristocratic and wealthy, and a grandfather had been a victor at Olympia in the horse-race. As he grew up, his city rose to become one of the leading places in the Greek world under the able leadership of the tyrant Theron. Theron had won a notable victory over the Carthaginians at the battle of Himera in 480, and used the spoils of victory to begin building the temples whose remains still astonish visitors to the site (near Agrigento in western Sicily). In a victory ode commemorating the Olympic success of one of its musicians, Pindar described Acragas as 'splendour-loving' and 'fairest of mortal cities'.

This was the brilliant back-drop against which Empedocles displayed his own remarkable talents in engineering, medicine, poetry, religious thought and, above all, philosophy. The self-portrait at the start of one of his works lacks nothing in pride and showmanship:

> My friends in the great city of Acragas ... I come among you as an immortal god, no longer a mortal, honoured by all as is my due, garlanded with the wreath of victory, and followed on my progress from city to city by admiring throngs of men and women in their thousands ...

In a more primitive community Empedocles would have been cast in the role of a 'medicine man'. The crowds who thronged to him were looking for prophecies and miracle cures. To the modern mind there is more than a touch of the charlatan about his claims to be able to control the winds, make or avert rain, and raise the dead to life. But he had substantial achievements to boast of. As a young man he played a leading part in the ejection of Theron's son from power and the establishment of a more democratic constitution. When the neighbouring city of Selinus was afflicted by a plague caused by pollution of its water supply, he cleansed the sources by the diversion of two streams into the main river. Above all, he brought his quick and passionate mind to bear on the twin problems of cosmology and personal salvation, and emerged as the leading thinker, after Parmenides, of the western Greek world. Given his life-style, the legend of his final apotheosis on Mt Etna was an almost inevitable outcome, but a more prosaic account records his death in exile in the Peloponnese.

Empedocles's fame rests on the surviving fragments of two great poems in hexameter verse, one entitled *On Nature* and the other *Purifications*. Of these we have 450 lines in all, perhaps about a tenth of the originals, but the most to survive from any of the Presocratics. *Purifications* deals with the nature and destiny of the soul, and is more religious in tone. *On Nature* shows a more scientific and philosophical approach.

Thought: the four Roots of things
On Nature contains some clear and deliberate echoes of Parmenides, showing that Empedocles must have been familiar with his work. He agrees that nothing is created from nothing, nor anything ultimately destroyed. He also rejects the concept of empty space. He accepts the logic of the Parmenidean contention that plurality cannot be derived from an original unity. But he firmly rejects the core of Parmenides's thought, namely, that All is One. Instead he posits an original multiplicity of basic elements.

Empedocles was a limited pluralist, holding that everything in the world is derived from four ultimate 'Roots': Fire, Air, Earth, Water. 'Roots' is his own term, a metaphor typical of his richly poetical style, and indicating his belief that the world of nature is something that grows and develops like a tree from a basic ground. The Ionian thinkers had variously supposed that one or other of these elements was more basic than the rest. The originality of

Empedocles lay in putting them on an equal footing as the primary elements of things.

Change as mixture

Having issued this direct challenge to Parmenidean Monism, Empedocles proceeded to tackle the problem of Change, whose reality had also been denied by Parmenides. His solution is summarised in the following quotation:

> These [the four Roots] exist in themselves, but running through one another they take on different appearances. To such an extent does the mingling interchange them.

At this point Empedocles explains his meaning by an effective simile taken from painting. He likens the four Roots to four basic colours on an artist's palette. These can be mixed to give any desired shade, and then applied to the canvas in patches of colour of varied shape or size. In this way the artist can produce an image of any and every object using only four basic pigments. He can do this because of the qualitative differences between the pigments, and also because they are able to 'run through' one another. In the same way, he supposed, the four elements possess qualitative differences and are infinitely combinable. It is these combinations which produce the various objects making up our world.

He observed, of course, that some substances mingle readily, such as water and wine, but others, for example, water and oil, do not. To explain such discrepancies he introduced the notion of 'passages' or 'channels' built into the structure of natural substances. When these 'passages' fitted one another like, say, hand and glove, commingling was easy, but the structures of water and oil made it difficult for them to coalesce. They were like the proverbial 'square pegs' and 'round holes'. The Greek for 'passage' is *poros* — hence English 'pore'. Following the lead of Empedocles, we still use 'pore' in physiological contexts, as when we speak of sweat exuded, or heat transmitted, through the 'pores' of the skin.

Theory of perception

Empedocles's theory of 'pores' was a novel and influential one. He used it in his explanation of perception, which in his view was due to a specific kind of mixing. He held that objects are continually emitting film-like portions of themselves, which he called 'effluences', from their surfaces, and when these mingle with our organs of sense they are absorbed and so perceived. A typically aristocratic interest in hunting is apparent in one perceptual example that he gives. Commenting on how hounds pick up the scent of game, he explains this as due to their absorption of 'fragments of the animal limbs' left on the vegetation where the game had passed. As Theophrastus saw, there has to be a 'symmetry' between the 'effluences' and the 'passages' in our body if the mixing called perception is to occur. We have, as it were, to be 'on the right channel' if we are to make contact with external reality.

Love and Strife as the cause of motion and change
Mixing obviously implies the motion of one element towards or through another, so Empedocles went on to consider the causes of motion. Here he was filling a gap left by his predecessors. The Milesians and Heraclitus just assumed that their first principle was capable of motion, and did not feel the need to assign any definite cause to explain motion. No explicit account of motion is attributed to the Pythagoreans. Parmenides dissolved the problem by denying the reality of motion. Empedocles attempted a positive solution, and showed his originality by positing two non-material principles, which he called Love and Strife, to account for motion, which in turn would explain the minglings and separations which take place in the world. He viewed Love and Strife as cosmic forces which function much as 'attraction' and 'repulsion' in modern scientific theory.

He believed that there is no absolute creation or destruction, but a never-ending cycle of change involving the four basic elements which respond to the powers of Love and Strife. Love overcomes the differences between the elements by attracting them together into a single whole. There is a creative aspect to this synthesis because it is productive of unity, but also a destructive aspect because individuality is submerged in the whole. Strife operates by accentuating basic differences, and so dissociating the elements by mutual repulsion. Obviously this destroys unity, but it also creates multiplicity, and enables individual objects such as men and animals and plants to come into existence.

Individual objects embody some or all of the four elements blended in different proportions. When they are compounded they may be said to come into existence, and when their elements are segregated, they may be said to perish. Empedocles is prepared to countenance a less precise or popular use of terms such as birth and death, provided it is realised that such terms do not apply to the elements, but only to the temporary compounds which we call things or creatures.

Empedocles considered that he could give an adequate explanation of the cosmos and its contents in terms of his four 'Roots' and two moving principles. But his explanation is far from being a deterministic one in terms of matter and motion. He allowed that organisms are frequently and casually produced from chance interactions of Love and Strife. For example, there is a bizarre fragment dealing with the 'monstrous' births which may result from an unsuitable mingling of forms in the one body. With regard to more normal organisms his view may have been that when a good proportion obtains between the various elements in a mixture serviceable compounds result. For instance, in the case of 'bone' there was a 'marvellous conjunction' of the elements of Earth, Water, and Fire in the proportion: two parts: two parts: four parts, and this is attributed to the action of Love. Aristotle accuses him of wavering between Chance and Purpose in his explanations, but given modern belief in a principle of indeterminacy, we can hardly say he was wrong to do so. In his account of the composition of 'blood' and 'flesh' he says: 'A roughly equal quantity of Earth fell in with [that is, by chance] roughly equal quantities of the three other elements...', in other words the proportion here is: 1:1:1:1.

The stages of the cosmic cycle

The forces of Love and Strife are not always in equilibrium. At times in the cosmic cycle Love gains complete ascendancy, and Strife is banished to the outermost fringe of the universe. We may call this Stage One. Empedocles called it the Sphere. He pictures the cosmos in this state as boundless and motionless, 'held fast in the dense obscurity of Love', and 'rejoicing in its circumambient stillness'. At this stage no separate sun can be discerned, and there is no distinction between earth and sea.

In Stage Two, Strife begins to re-enter the Sphere, bringing motion with it. As Empedocles graphically puts it: 'All the limbs of the god began to quiver in turn.' The cause of this change is the 'broad oath' of Necessity. In other words, a principle of cosmic justice requires that neither Love nor Strife shall gain a permanent ascendancy, but each shall yield victory in turn to the other. The elements now begin to draw apart, with Fire moving up into the heavens, and Earth and Water sinking down, but manifestations of volcanic fire from below the earth's surface show that there is still much admixture. Our world is at this stage of advancing Strife.

Stage Three sees Strife triumphant with Love totally banished, and Stage Four is the period when Love gradually reasserts its influence. Neither of these stages is clearly pictured in the extant fragments, but their outline at least can be inferred from what is said about the first two stages, and they are necessary to complete the overall picture of an endless alternating cycle of cosmic change. The picture is typical of the comprehensive grandeur of much Presocratic thought, and is not without parallel in some modern cosmologies, where an expanding universe alternates with a period of cosmic contraction.

The nature and destiny of the soul

From the scientific point of view Empedocles regards 'soul' as an inherent 'life principle' operative in perception and thought. It is composed of all four elements, and also contains the forces of Love and Strife. This enables it to recognise and respond to these same elements and forces in the outside world. However, most of what Empedocles says about the soul comes from the poem *Purifications*, and is designed to account for the 'fallen' state of human souls, and to explain how they may regain a lost state of bliss. In our terms the doctrine is theological rather than scientific, but Empedocles probably did not recognise any distinction between the cosmos and 'the divine'.

The soul, then, is an immortal spirit whose natural abode is with the blessed ones, but it has been seduced into sin by Strife, and is now 'in exile' from the heavenly regions. The condition of this exile condemns it to repeated incarnations in human, animal, and even plant form. Empedocles makes it clear that these reincarnations constitute a punishment for something like 'original sin', a sin connected with the taking of life. Just as the ancient punishment for homicide was banishment, so the soul becomes 'an exile from god and a wanderer'. The offending soul is an object of hate to the elements, and they reject it, tossing it in turn from one to the other.

To earn its release from these miseries the soul must turn, like the men of the Golden Age, to the worship and service of Aphrodite

(Love). In a remarkable passage he looks back to the time before the rule of Zeus or Kronos when 'the Cyprian Goddess was queen', worshipped with offerings of honey, frankincense, and myrrh, and 'the altar was not bedewed with the pure blood of bulls'. It now becomes clear that Empedocles was a passionate vegetarian. This is what the rule of Love requires. It was Strife that led to the first taking of life. The eating of flesh is stigmatised as a 'terrible deed', and animal sacrifice is viewed as akin to the murder of a close relative. The first step on the road to salvation is to abstain from such sacrifices, and also from animal food. One must then go on to practise the prescribed rituals of purification, to 'fast from evil' — a striking phrase — and to acquire a knowledge of the divine realm.

It should be clear from this summary that there are four main points of contact between *Purifications* and *On Nature*. First, the 'reign of Aphrodite' is to be equated with that time in the cosmic cycle when Love is supreme and Strife has been banished from the world. Secondly, reincarnation is set in the context of the four elements which have been segregated by Strife, and so are hostile to the embodied spirit. Thirdly, the moral struggle is interpreted as a consistent attempt to re-enthrone Love among all animate beings. Fourthly, and finally, philosophical insight is itself seen to be the most important form of purification, and it is the souls of the wise who become gods. His remarkable saying 'Blessed is he who has acquired the wealth of divine thoughts' will serve as a fitting epitaph for this gifted and idiosyncratic Sicilian thinker.

ANAXAGORAS

Life and writings

Anaxagoras of Clazomenae (*c.*500–428) was born into a wealthy family but played no part in the commerce or politics of his native city. Much of his life was spent abroad, particularly in Athens. His first visit to that city may have been an enforced one as a conscript in the Persian army which invaded Greece in 480. Later he resided there for thirty years (perhaps not continuously), and became the teacher and friend of its leading statesman, Pericles. Pericles's natural talent for oratory was said to have been raised to perfection through his philosophical discussions with Anaxagoras which elevated his thoughts and freed his mind from popular superstitions.

The rational cast of Anaxagoras's mind is well illustrated by an anecdote in Plutarch's *Life of Pericles*. The skull of a ram with a single well-formed horn in the centre of its forehead was sent in from the Attic countryside and brought to Pericles's attention as a portent. A soothsayer called Lampon was summoned, and he interpreted it as a sign that Pericles would soon oust a rival and gain sole power in the city. Anaxagoras used a very different approach. He opened up the skull and pointed out that the marrow in the brain cavity had drawn together into an egg-shaped mass with the point at the base of the horn. The malformation, he suggested, was simply due to this anatomical anomaly. The people, however, thought that Lampon had given the better explanation since the rival did indeed fall from power soon afterwards.

After the start of the Peloponnesian War in 431 Pericles lost popularity, and his enemies tried to erode his position by a series of attacks on his friends and associates. Anaxagoras was one of the first to suffer. He was alleged to have contravened a recent decree which forbade anyone to disregard the supernatural or give instruction about the heavenly bodies. Under threat of prosecution for the 'impiety' of his scientific outlook, Anaxagoras was forced to leave Athens, and he emigrated to Lampsacus on the Sea of Marmara, where he is said to have founded a philosophical school. He won the respect of the people of Lampsacus, and when they asked him on his death-bed how he would like to be commemorated, he requested that an annual holiday should be given to the school-children in his memory. The citizens of Clazomenae did not forget him either, and in later times a representation of him appeared on their coins—a rare distinction for a philosopher.

Anaxagoras had a very significant influence on the intellectual life of Athens. He was the first major philosopher to reside there, and through his Athenian pupil Archelaus Ionian scientific speculation became naturalised in the city. The effect was felt by minds as diverse as those of Socrates and Euripides. Anaxagoras's thought was totally apolitical. He became the type of the lofty-minded thinker with a soul far above all mundane matters. He is said to have made over his property to his relatives, and when someone asked him, 'Have you no care for your country?' he replied, 'I have a great care for my country', *pointing to the sky*. This anecdote marks him out as the first explicit 'cosmopolitan', that is to say, 'citizen of the universe' owing allegiance to scientific truth rather than to

Athens or Clazomenae. The immense reach of his intellect is seen in his reply to a doubtless sarcastic enquiry by a man of Lampsacus as to whether the moutains surrounding that city would ever turn into sea; 'Yes,' he said, 'provided that time does not fail.'

Anaxagoras was the intellectual heir *par excellence* of the early Milesian thinkers, a life-long devotee of 'free enquiry' (*historia**). Very different in temperament from the passionate Empedocles, he composed his great work on the *Nature of the World* in prose rather than verse. A number of key extracts survive, enabling us to reconstruct his system with a fair measure of confidence.

Thought: Mind and motion

Anaxagoras was the first thinker to attach major importance to the role of Mind in the formation of the world. Aristotle regarded this as a decisive philosophical advance, and commends Anaxagoras as the first 'sober' thinker after a succession of 'babblers'. The sobriety, and indeed dignity, of Anaxagoras's thought on this topic comes across in the following extract from his book:

> Other things share in a portion of all things, but Mind is boundless and rules itself, and is mingled with no other thing, but remains apart by itself. For if it were not apart but had been mixed with any other thing, it would have shared in everything if it had been mixed with anything. For, as I have said above, there is a portion of everything in everything. And if other things had been mixed with Mind they would have prevented it from exercising the rule which it does when apart by itself. For Mind is the slenderest and purest of all things. Mind is the ruling force in all things that have life whether greater or smaller.

Mind existing apart from things, and so in control of things, was, in Anaxagoras's view, the originating cause of motion in the universe. The first motion was circular, and on a limited scale, a primal vortex inserted by Mind into pre-existent chaos. As the motion spread and gathered speed recognisable entities began to separate out from the primeval mixture. The dense separated from the rare, the hot from the cold, the bright from the dark, and the dry from the moist. An ordered world appeared, whose main constituents are earth and sky, sea and dry land, and whose most striking objects are the heavenly bodies that circle constantly overhead.

In the first chapter of the Hebrew Bible we read how in the beginning 'the earth was without form, and void' and how 'God divided the light from the darkness' and 'the waters from the waters'. The concept is similar, but the mechanism is different. In the religious account the creator God calls things into existence by the power of his word. In the theory of Anaxagoras Mind initiates motion, and motion then takes over as the driving force by which an ordered world is produced. Genesis is inherently theological, Anaxagoras recognisably scientific. The two accounts have something in common in that both tend to emphasise the otherness of a controlling principle that pre-dates the cosmos and comprehends it as it comes into existence. But in the end they part company because Anaxagoras denies the possibility of creation *ex nihilo*.

> The Greeks have an incorrect understanding of 'creation' and 'destruction'. Nothing is created or destroyed, but things are made or unmade by the mingling or dispersal of [already] existent things.

Plato tells us that Socrates was impressed by what Anaxagoras had to say about Mind, but criticised him for failing to make full use of Mind as the ordering cause of things. Even without this evidence we could detect a lack of 'follow-through' in the extant fragments. If Mind knows and controls all things even before they are separated out from the primeval chaos, as Anaxagoras says it does, it would seem to be logical to make it the Intelligent Designer of all things. But Anaxagoras does not seem to have taken this step. Instead he stresses repeatedly 'separation through motion', that is, a mechanical cause, as the effective agent in producing the world of distinguishable objects in which we live.

Matter

If Anaxagoras's theory of Mind is fairly straightforward, his views on the nature of material objects are notoriously subtle and complex. One may begin the exposition from the trenchant fragment:

> The world is one world, and there is no gap between the things in it, no axe-cut separating hot from cold or cold from hot.

This affirmation of the present togetherness of things is further amplified by his statement that:

There is a portion of everything in everything.

The doctrine is logically coherent with his conception of an antecedent 'chaos' in which all the constituents of matter were inextricably mingled together. In this motionless mass he envisaged the 'seeds' of things as so thoroughly jumbled up together that no colours could be perceived, and hence no distinct objects identified by sight. (To illustrate this thought one might compare the dull muddy liquid that results when all the separate pigments in a paint-box are mixed together on the same palette.)

His introduction of 'seed' as a new technical term for material element is very significant, and testifies to his interest in biological process. The growth of a large tree from a tiny seed might well be regarded as the appearance of something new in the world. But since Anaxagoras in effect believes that the sum-total of matter is constant he cannot allow that the trunk and leaves are really new. The separately perceived parts of the grown tree are, in his view, simply larger aggregates of constituent elements ('portions') that were already present in the seed. The tree increases in bulk by assimilating similar constituents from the soil in which it is rooted, or the water and air with which it comes in contact.

He would have given a similar account of the growth of an animal from seed through embryo to fully developed specimen. 'How', he pertinently asks, 'could hair come from what is not hair, and flesh from what is not flesh?' Modern nutritionists might well ask the same question, and their answer would turn on protein in food converted into protein in the animal's tissues. They are philosophically at one with Anaxagoras, differing only in their much more thorough grasp of the chemical processes of the transformation.

Homoeomerous parts

It is time to introduce the most difficult part of Anaxagoras's doctrine of matter: the concept of 'homoeomereity' (*homoiomereia**). The term embodies two Greek roots meaning 'similar' and 'part'. It occurs in doxographical accounts of his system, not in the extant fragments, and may be a later coinage to express one very distinctive aspect of his theory.

Anaxagoras maintained that every portion of the material world, no matter how small, contains all the constituents that are distinguishable in any larger portion. How then is one object different from another? The answer lies in the principle of *preponderance*. In the mixture of constituent qualities that constitute a distinct object we perceive only those that preponderate in it as a whole, or (in the case of sight) cluster on its surface. We say that the apple is red, forgetting its white interior. We call it sweet, but its core is bitter. Its skin is soft to the touch, but its pips are hard. The apple is a 'homoeomerous' thing in the sense that a total inventory of its 'parts' would be an inventory of all the 'parts' that there are.

In the case of the 'parts' of a nugget of gold, the inventory would be the same as for the apple, but the proportions of the various items different. In gold, hard, heavy, and dry 'parts' preponderate, giving it very different sensible qualities. The same analysis applies to anything we call a 'thing'. We would consider gold to be a homogeneous substance, and we can accept that even a speck of gold will have the same constituents as a gold bar. In the same way a splinter of bone will have the same constituents as a complete bone. The term 'homoeomerous' is used to express this feature of things also. It can mean 'a thing whose every part is similar to every other part of the same thing'. But it also bears the larger and more paradoxical meaning of 'a thing having parts similar to the parts of everything else'. As Anaxagoras emphasises: 'There is a portion of everything in everything.'

The word 'portion' seems to express his thought better than 'part'. 'Part' tends to suggest separate particles, but the 'things' in Anaxagoras's world are *not* composed of separate particles. They should rather be conceived as collections of blended 'stuffs', much as a beam of white light may be viewed as a blend of all the colours of the rainbow. With the aid of a prism we can 'separate out' the various colours mechanically, and that is one way in which things can be changed. But his theory can also allow for more complicated types of 'extraction' as when the stuff of hair is extracted by chemical transformation from the food we ingest. Impressed by the immense variety of such transformations he was prepared to allow that in theory anything can change into anything, given the infinite variety of 'portions' inherent in everything.

It remains to summarise the more abstract and mathematical aspects of Anaxagoras's theory of matter. He conceived of the material world as a continuum which is infinitely divisible in fact as in thought, but no matter how small a portion is imagined, there is still an infinity of parts within 'the small'. There is no 'least part' of anything, for this would imply a rent in the seamless robe of things. Similarly matter is indefinitely extensible. There is no empty space bounding a finite universe. There is an infinity without, just as there is an infinity within, and these infinities are 'equal'. Modern commentators have rightly praised him for his sophisticated grasp of the theory of infinite sets.

All the above points are made or implied in the extant fragments. They could represent a polemical attack on Zeno's denial of plurality, or on the Pythagorean conception of 'unit-points', but this is far from certain. The relationship of Anaxagoras to Parmenides is clearer. He agrees with his great predecessor that there is no empty space, and no creation *ex nihilo*, but rejects his motionless One. By positing an infinite number of infinitely varied 'seeds' of things, initially at rest, but then stirred into motion by Mind, he is able to account for the diversity of moving and changing objects in the world that we humans perceive around us. His system possesses a subtle vitality, and must be taken seriously as a plausible outline account of the true nature of materiality.

GENERAL CONCLUSION

Empedocles was a unique individualist who founded no school. His system was quite well regarded by Aristotle probably because he made a brave attempt to explain cosmic motion and change in terms of what would now be called 'attraction' and 'repulsion'. The limited pluralism of his four Roots had only a limited appeal and did not generate any new cosmological thinking. On the other hand his theory of 'pores' and 'effluences' was taken up by the Atomists and became the received account for centuries.

Anaxagoras had some followers, notably Archelaus, a friend of Socrates, who introduced Ionian science to Athens. He received unusually high praise from Aristotle for his pioneering concept of a cosmic Mind. His theory of matter was too subtle and difficult for his contemporaries and made no lasting impact.

Neither thinker initiated any major line of development in the understanding of the natural world. The main line of progess lay in the adoption of Eleatic Monism by the Ionian Melissus, and in the strong reaction which he seems to have provoked in the Atomists Leucippus and Democritus.

6

FROM MONISM TO ATOMISM

AFTER THE Persian conquest of Greek Asia Minor the current of philosophy flowed westwards from Ionia to Italy, and found a new centre in Elea. But in the generation after Parmenides that trend was reversed. From Elea the influence of Parmenidean Monism flowed back again to the Aegean, and a second Samian appeared briefly on the stage of philosophical history. This was Melissus (c.480–420), who reaffirmed Monism, and so in effect denied that Empedocles and Anaxagoras had found a satisfactory way to circumvent Parmenides's arguments against motion and change.

If philosophy was to advance, a new way had to be found, but Melissus was not the man to find it. His main significance in the history of thought lies in the fact that his forceful up-dating of the monistic hypothesis in good Ionian prose (considerable fragments of which are extant) apparently provoked two other brilliant Ionians to found and develop the theory of Atomism. The story of how this advance came about is outlined in the present chapter.

Lives and writings of Leucippus and Democritus

Leucippus and Democritus were both connected with Abdera, a somewhat unimportant Ionian colony in northern Greece. Democritus was a native of the place, and there is a good tradition about his life and writings. Leucippus remains a more shadowy figure, and doubt has even been cast on his existence, but such doubt is misplaced. We may reasonably infer from our sources that he was born in Miletus c.470, that he travelled to Elea to study under Zeno, and that he finally founded a school in Abdera, where Democritus became his pupil. He should be recognised as the senior partner in a great joint enterprise — the building of the ancient atomic system. He came to be over-shadowed by Democritus, so much so that only one sentence survives from the two books attributed to him, but he was probably the pioneer in developing the principles on which the system was based. These would have been set out in his book entitled *Great World System*, which may have appeared c.430.

Democritus was born c.460, and seems to have long out-lived his senior colleague, reportedly becoming a centenarian. He had a typically Ionian zest for wide-ranging enquiry, and the most diverse interests are reflected in his numerous writings. We have the titles of over sixty works, covering a wide range of topics. From this encyclopaedic output many short citations amounting to some 300 fragments in all survive, but the works themselves have perished. It is especially regrettable that so little survives from his *Little World System* which is believed to have contained a comprehensive exposition of the origin of the world, the genesis of animals, and the cultural history of mankind. His development of Atomism was his most significant contribution to the progress of philosophy, but virtually nothing on this aspect of his thought survives in his own words. However, he was the major influence on Epicurus, and the main outlines of his physical theory are recoverable from the latter's system.

The atomic hypothesis

Leucippus, according to Aristotle, arrived at the atomic hypothesis from a consideration of motion and the void (empty space) in an Eleatic context. Melissus had explicitly rejected the existence of empty space, and with it the possibility of motion. Leucippus tried a totally different approach. He wanted to justify motion, and so he posited that there *is* empty space and that bodies can and do move in it.

This was his significant initial move. It was not intended as a total rejection of Eleatic doctrine. He agreed that being has an integrity which excludes not-being in the sense that what exists is full and complete, and totally excludes what is empty. But his next move, again probably stimulated by opposition to Melissus, represented a radical undermining of Monism.

Melissus had used a neat *reductio ad absurdum* argument for the unity of being. 'If things were many,' he had urged, 'they would have to be such as I affirm the one to be.' Melissus concluded that this was impossible, for plurality could not co-exist with unified being. Leucippus in effect said: Why not? He claimed that 'what is' consists of an infinite plurality of entities, each too small to be seen, but each possessing some bulk, and each endowed with the salient characteristics of the Eleatic One, especially indestructibility.

Thus was born the concept of the 'atom' (*atomon**), a Greek term meaning 'that which cannot be cut'. Indivisibility was a property of the One, as emphasised by Parmenides, so this became a central property of the Leucippan atom, rendering it immune from internal change. How then does change take place? Leucippus had a plausible answer. As the atoms move in the void, they collide, rebound, and interlock, and so come together to form larger aggregates which can be perceived by the senses. Visible and tangible things are produced by the chance association of atoms, and when the collection of atoms which *we* call a 'thing' breaks up and dissolves back into the void the 'thing' is destroyed. But no individual atom is destroyed in the process. In this most ingenious way the permanence of Eleatic being was combined with the common-sense notions of plurality, movement, and change, and the atomic theory of matter came into existence.

The theory was then developed jointly by Leucippus and Democritus, and it is seldom possible on the evidence to separate their contributions. They held that all atoms are alike in substance, but differ in *shape*. This difference in shape is an important factor in generating differences between sensible objects formed from collections of atoms.

The point was neatly illustrated by comparing the letters A and N, each different in outline, but both composed of three straight lines. Differences between things, they held, were also caused by two other factors in the lining up of the atoms, which they called 'mutual contact' and 'turning'. These terms seem to have been chosen to emphasise the dynamic nature of atomic interaction. They were later replaced by the less colourful 'arrangement' and 'position', terms also illustrated by the letter comparison. AN differs from NA in *arrangement*, and Z from N in *position*. It is worth pointing out that in Latin the same word *elementum* does duty for 'letter' and (physical) 'element'. The example of the alphabet reminds us that a limited number of simple shapes in combination can be used to convey an infinitude of meanings. In the same way the Atomists believed that the infinite variety of the sensible world is basically produced by differences in the shape, arrangement, and positioning of the atoms.

The analogy of the alphabet must not be pressed too far. Its letters are limited both in number and shape, but this was not the case with the atoms. They were held to be unlimited in number and shape, and they were probably also conceived as varying indefinitely in size, though within microscopic limits. The importance of their variations in shape is emphasised by the fact that Democritus wrote a work entitled 'On Forms', meaning 'On Atoms'.

Unlike the 'seeds' of Anaxagoras or the 'roots' of Empedocles, the atoms were not thought to have qualities such as colour or smell or flavour. These 'secondary' qualities, as they later came to be called, were not part of the external physical world in the same way as 'shape' or 'extension', which were 'primary' because they belonged to the atoms themselves. However, the primary quality of shape was used to explain a secondary quality like flavour, which became evident to the taste when the atoms were ingested in food. For example, a 'sharp' flavour was said to come from atoms with an angular and fretted shape, and 'sweetness' from shapes that were rounded and not too small.

Cosmology

The modern catch-phrase 'worlds in collision' was strikingly anticipated by Democritus. As reported by Hippolytus, he held that the concourse of an infinite number of atoms in space was bound to produce 'innumerable worlds differing in size'. The extract continues in a way which might well be termed the original blue-print for space fiction:

> In some of these worlds there is no sun or moon, in some they are larger than our sun and moon, and in some there are several suns and moons. The intervals between these worlds are irregular, and in some directions they are more numerous, in others less. In one place they are being born, in another dying. Some of them are growing, some are in their prime, and some are declining. *When they collide they destroy one another.* There are some worlds which are devoid of animals and plants, and completely waterless.

A coherent scheme of world-formation is attributed to Leucippus by Diogenes, and the main points from it are as follows: When a great mass of atoms streams into a 'great void', a single circular motion is set up (the vortex principle). It is this common circular motion, replacing the previous random movements of individual atoms, that lies at the root of an ordered world. The whirl of the mass ejects the smallest atoms into the void without, but the remainder are sorted on the principle of 'like to like', like 'pebbles on a beach', and come together to form a 'spherical complex'. This complex contains a great variety of atoms enclosed within a separate envelope which is compared to a 'membrane' or 'caul'. The eddying motion continues, and, as in a whirlpool, heavier bodies collect in the centre to form an 'earth'. The surrounding membrane then becomes thin, but because of its faster rotation it picks up additional particles. Some of these form a complex that is 'wet and muddy' at first, but dries out as it spins, and finally ignites to form the substance of the stars.

It is clear that these remarkable speculations are designed to exclude all hint of purpose from the formation of our world. There is no cosmic Mind at work as in the system of Anaxagoras, no Love and Strife as in Empedocles. Atomic matter and mechanical motion underpin the whole scheme. It seems that a critical mass of atoms must come together in a given region for the 'whirl' to commence. We are not told why this happens, but once it does the vortex imposes itself on the mass and the rest of the process seems to follow of necessity. As Leucippus tells us in the one sentence to survive from his writings: 'Nothing comes into existence at random, but there is an explanation for everything, and everything is brought into being by necessity.' This famous dictum still stands as the guiding light of scientific enquiry. A similar spirit infuses a stray remark of Democritus preserved in a late Christian source: 'I would rather discover one causal explanation than possess the kingdom of Persia.'

Theory of knowledge
The Atomists aimed at giving an objective and scientific account of the universe, but paradoxically the roots of scepticism were inherent in their doctrine that the basic constituents of things are devoid of qualities like colour or smell. How then is one to react when confronted by the blue of the sky and the green of the grass? Are all such data subjective or illusory? Democritus's reaction was to attempt to draw a firm line between the 'conventional', that is, what is believed to be the case, and the 'real', that is, what actually is the case. We may believe and say that the grass is green, but reason tells

us that the colour is only in our eye. The reality consists of colourless and invisible atoms. This view was summed up in a much quoted dictum:

> By convention 'sweet', by convention 'bitter', by convention 'hot', by convention 'cold', by convention 'colour'; but in reality, atoms and void.

But once doubt is cast on the reliability of the senses, the seeds of scepticism are well and truly sown. These bore fruit in the work of one of his pupils, Metrodorus of Chios, who began his book *On Nature* with the assertion: 'None of us knows anything...'

Democritus must have realised that he was on a slippery slope. There is a dramatic fragment in which he represents the senses remonstrating with the intellect:

> Wretched Intellect, are you trying to overturn us with proofs that we have provided? Our overthrow is your fall.

This indicates a realisation of the problems that arise for science if it rejects the evidence of the senses, and it seems that he tried to stop well short of total scepticism by drawing a distinction between 'bastard' knowledge and 'genuine' knowledge. The senses were channels admitting a 'bastard' form of knowledge, which may be identified with 'opinion', and which could presumably be 'right opinion', just as a bastard may be a good man though his parentage is dubious. Genuine knowledge came through reasoning, and could not be erroneous because it represented an impeccable union between the mind and external reality.

Conclusion

Atomism marked the culmination of the materialistic trend in Presocratic thought. It claimed to explain all phenomena in terms of matter, space, and motion — a most elegant and economical hypothesis. The validity of the theory was strongly denied by Plato and Aristotle, but it survived to form the speculative basis for the Epicurean system of physics. In later antiquity and the mediaeval period it was despised by Neoplatonists and Christians alike, but though it sank into disrepute it was never totally forgotten. Renaissance scholarship promoted its revival as a coherent account of the physical world, and in the middle of the seventeenth century it received a strong endorsement in the work of the French philosopher-scientist Gassendi. Since that time it has slipped easily into place as an essential part of the conceptual basis of modern science. Ancient atomic theory amounted to a strong affirmation of the view that the ultimate structure of matter consists of separate particles. Despite its vast complexity and sophistication, modern nuclear physics also seems wedded to a particulate view of material entities.

7

HUMANISM AND ENLIGHTENMENT: THE SOPHISTS AND SOCRATES

BY THE MIDDLE of the fifth century BC a marked change is detectable in the cultural and intellectual life of the Greek world. The transformation was only partly due to the progress of philosophy. Developments in this narrower field now began to coalesce and interact with broader political and educational advances to produce a brilliant and intellectually varied epoch of Enlightenment, which may be taken to extend down to the end of the century, but whose effects were much more long-lasting.

This Greek Enlightenment found its brightest and sharpest focus in Periclean Athens. As a movement it had much in common with its eighteenth-century European counterpart. It was an age of doubt and questioning, but also an age when humanistic values were strenuously and persuasively advocated by influential thinkers. The movement gained strength against a background of increasing freedom for the individual, particularly in Athens and the other cities which copied her democratic institutions. It was an intellectual movement which became increasingly critical of authority and convention. A serious rift began to open up between traditional religious belief and progressive Ionian science, causing concern to conservative politicians. But in general the movement was less concerned with the world of nature and more interested in the world of human affairs. It was chiefly fuelled and forwarded by a group of teachers called Sophists, whose main aim was to help their pupils to achieve success in public life rather than in theoretical speculation.

THE SOPHISTS

The rise of the Sophistic movement

The Sophists were a new breed of educators who now began to appear in many parts of the Greek world. The word *sophistes** had long been used as a general term to designate people who were both wise and skilled. It could equally well be applied to poets and carpenters, doctors and statesmen. But from about 450 onwards it came more and more to be the approved label for wandering 'professors' who travelled from city to city offering courses of instruction in a wide variety of subjects. These 'professors' would teach through public lecture or private seminar, and expected to be, and were, well paid for their trouble. Nothing like them had been seen in Greece before. They were a new professional class responding to a new demand for higher education.

The oldest and most famous of the Sophists was Protagoras of Abdera (*c*.490–420), who was said to have been the first to accept fees for his tuition. In Plato's dialogue *Protagoras* he is depicted as claiming to teach 'excellence', and his programme is defined as offering 'good counsel in family matters, namely the expert management of one's own household, and good counsel in public matters, namely how to contribute most effectively by speech and action in the affairs of the city'. In former times such instruction would have been passed on informally by precept and example from the heads of leading families to their sons, but now the young aristocrats of progressive states like Athens were looking for something more up to date and professional, and this was the need to which Protagoras and his fellow-Sophists catered.

The opening was made for them by rising expectations in Greek education generally, and by the advance of democracy, Athenian-style, in particular. As political power tended to become concentrated in large popular assemblies and juries, the art of effective public speaking stood at an ever higher premium, and would-be politicians were willing to pay high fees to anyone who could impart it.

The Sophists were well able to demonstrate their expertise, and a notable instance of this occurred when Gorgias of Leontini (*c*.483–376) was sent to Athens in 427 to plead his city's case against Syracuse. His oration with its rhythmic cadences so enthralled the Athenians that it set a new fashion in public speaking, and Gorgias won so much favourable publicity that he was able to stay on and give a profitable series of courses in rhetoric.

In Athens the legal system was often used for making attacks on political opponents. The courts became wordy battle-grounds, and more effective methods of pleading cases and presenting arguments were studied and taught by the Sophists. Protagoras set the fashion here with a treatise entitled *Controversial Arguing*. This type of instruction tended to get the new education a bad name. As Aristophanes put it in the *Clouds*, the Sophists were regarded as past-masters in the art of 'making the worse appear the better cause' — hence the modern sense of 'sophistry'. Gorgias denied that there was anything reprehensible in teaching speech skills. They were, he said, morally neutral, and would not be criticised if always put to good ends. His own brother was a doctor and would call him in to persuade his more timid patients to submit to surgical treatment. This in Gorgias's view was a good use of rhetoric and showed the practical superiority of what he well defined as 'the art of persuasion'. He should not, he argued, be held responsible for any misuse of the art by less scrupulous pupils.

The bulk of the work of the Sophists was done through pupil-contact, but they also wrote manuals and text-books. Thus were produced the first grammars and the first hand-books of rhetoric and literary criticism. These have not survived, since they were at rather an elementary level and were later superseded by more advanced works, but at the time they represented an important pioneering element in formal Greek education. They are also significant as representing the stage in linguistic development when language first became conscious of itself, and started to reflect on, and describe, its own operations.

Philosophical aspects of the Sophistic movement

(A) Humanism

The early Sophists were great individualists, and it would be wrong to regard them as members of one philosophical school sharing the same doctrines. However, it is possible to discern a common tendency in their thought and educational practice. This tendency is well summed up in one of the very few sentences to survive from the writings of Protagoras. He began his work entitled *Truth* with the memorable dictum:

81

> Man is the measure of all things, of the existence of what exists, and of the non-existence of what does not exist.

This famous sentence is rightly regarded as the key manifesto of Greek humanism. If 'man' means 'each individual human being' (rather than 'mankind in general' as some take it) the dictum in effect draws a line round a person with his personal concerns and assures him that he is the best judge of truth in that particular area. It put a premium on individual judgement, thus favouring the trends of the time towards democracy and egalitarianism. It also represented a plea for tolerance and freedom of opinion. If challenged to state his view of 'truth' Protagoras would probably have taken the pragmatic line that truth consists in beliefs or opinions which work to the benefit of an individual or a community.

The dictum also implies that certain matters are too lofty for human beings to form a valid opinion about them. This agnostic attitude is well illustrated by another saying of Protagoras:

> I am unable to reach knowledge about the gods, either that they exist, or do not exist, or of their essential nature. Among the many factors which prevent me from knowing are the obscurity of the subject and the shortness of human life.

In general the Sophists turned away from scientific speculation about Nature and philosophical preoccupation with ultimate Reality, and concentrated on subjects that seemed to have direct relevance to the conduct of human life. They discussed the basis of law and morality, and argued the merits of different political systems, thus laying the foundations for the systematic study of ethics and politics. Most of the issues they raised are still live today. At their best they were champions of human rights, and some even questioned the validity of the deep-rooted social institution of slavery.

(B) Relativism
Their intense involvement in humanistic disciplines made them only too well aware of the volatile nature of opinion, and their wandering way of life brought home to them the variability of custom from one society to another. Herodotus also appreciated such considerations from his own travels and researches, and he tells a typical 'enlightenment' story about human burial customs. King Darius, he says, asked some Greeks who were present at his

court whether they could be induced by a large bribe to dispose of their dead parents by eating them, and they replied that no consideration could ever induce them to do so. He then summoned a tribe of Indians whose custom was to do just this, and asked them could they be induced to cremate them instead, and they cried out in horror at the impiety of the suggestion. Herodotus concludes that Pindar was right to say: 'Custom is King.' The moral of the story in his view is that one should be tolerant of other people's customs no matter how repulsive they seem, because every group inevitably thinks that its own ways are best. Other thinkers, particularly second-generation Sophists and circles influenced by them, drew a more corrosive conclusion from such instances. It seemed to them that if there was no common or natural basis for custom, there could be no absolute standards in morality, and from this it was a short step to the view that moral restraints were merely conventional, and so contrary to nature.

A hasty reading of Plato has often given the impression that the Sophists had a corrupting influence on public morality. If public morality did decline in fifth-century Greece, which is not easy to prove, the reasons were much more complex. Men like Protagoras and Gorgias could never have gained the respect they did if they had openly tried to subvert the moral standards of their pupils. And there is in fact good positive evidence that they argued powerfully for traditional methods of character-building and accepted standards of decent conduct. But the spirit of the age was anti-authoritarian, and religious belief was being questioned, if not attacked. Some later and less distinguished Sophists, such as Thrasymachus who figures in Plato's *Republic*, did adopt distinctly amoral views, but they may have been following rather than moulding social attitudes already corrupted by civic strife and the long disastrous war between Athens and Sparta.

(C) Scepticism and atheism
The rise of philosophy was itself a factor in the growth of sceptical trends. Attention has already been drawn to certain negative factors inherent in Eleaticism. Parmenides's concentration on pure reason undermined confidence in the senses, and Zeno's destructive use of dialectical argument showed how difficult it was to maintain the truth of any proposition. In addition, when keen minds began to take stock of a century and more of philosophical speculation, it was

all too easy for them to conclude that the development of the subject had produced more dissension than agreement.

Disenchantment with abstract reasoning is apparent in a work of Gorgias entitled *On the Non-existent or On Nature*. The work itself has not survived, but two extant paraphrases enable its reconstruction in considerable detail. Gorgias argued: (1) that nothing exists; (2) that even if anything exists, it cannot be apprehended by man; (3) that even if anything can be apprehended, it cannot be expressed or communicated to another.

There is an element of parody and sophism in the work, but it was also seriously meant as a rejection of the one true Being posited by Parmenides. There is, says Gorgias in effect, no non-sensible reality lying behind appearance, no thing-in-itself. And even if there were such a reality, no man could know it, think it, or describe it. Each man is locked into the private world of what appears to his senses to be the case. Philosophical scepticism and subjectivism could hardly go further than this, and the position is probably inconsistent with any educational enterprise. But Gorgias was at least well aware of the difficulty of attaining objective truth. There is an eloquent but melancholy expression of this in one of his extant rhetorical exercises called the *Helen*:

> It is no easy matter to remember the past, consider the present, or divine the future. So in most matters most people take opinion as their mind's adviser. But opinion being uncertain and insecure shields those who rely on it with forms of happiness that are also uncertain and insecure.

Parallel with Gorgias's rejection of metaphysics went a widespread rejection of religious dogma. In the *Clouds* of Aristophanes (produced in 423) a stage Socrates tells his prospective pupil Strepsiades that 'the gods are no longer current coin in my school', and after some elementary tuition in meteorology Strepsiades agrees that 'Zeus is no more, and Vortex is King'. This is a travesty of Socrates's real views, but an accurate enough reflection of the freethinking encouraged in Athens by the blending of Ionian science with Sophistic education. As the century wore on, the pragmatic agnosticism expressed by Protagoras was replaced by a more aggressive type of atheism.

Atheism was particularly associated in the Athenian mind with a certain Diagoras of Melos, surnamed 'the godless', who was convicted on a charge of impiety. We do not know what arguments Diagoras used, but a positivist account of the origin of belief in the gods is attributed to another famous Sophist, Prodicus of Ceos (dates uncertain). He is said to have maintained that the received gods were originally either culture-heroes who made useful discoveries like corn-growing, or the actual products, like wheat or bread, which sustained life and so received the respect and worship of primitive peoples. On this view Demeter would be either the discoverer of wheat or the wheat itself, Dionysus the discoverer of viniculture or the wine itself, and so on. This account is typical of the then current anthropological speculation which rejected the traditional account of man's decline from a Golden Age, and stressed instead how human beings had raised themselves from primitive savagery by their own exertions and resourcefulness.

A characteristic of such speculation was the view that law and order represented a secondary phase in the evolution of society. Laws, it was held, lacked any basis in nature, and only arose as the result of a convention or contract between members of a social group when the consequences of anarchy proved too unpalatable.

An even more cynical twist to this line of thought was supplied by the Athenian Critias (*c*.460–403). In one of his plays he made a character argue that the notion of an all-seeing, all-knowing deity was simply a fiction invented by some clever statesman to 'put the fear of god' into wrong-doers. Such radical freethinking was an extreme end-product of what had started as a laudable movement towards a more open and enlightened society. It typified the sceptical and anarchic tendencies inherent in more sophisticated forms of education. One can easily see why the Sophistic movement provoked strong reactions among ordinary people, among conservative politicians, and among the keenest philosophical minds. But nowhere was this reaction more intense and significant than in the life and work of Socrates, to whom I now turn.

SOCRATES

Life and activities

Socrates (469–399) was born into an urban Athenian family of modest means. His mother was a mid-wife, his father a sculptor, and that was Socrates's trade too, but he never worked much at it, and was regarded as a poor man, although he did marry and raise a family. Hardly ever leaving Athens except to go on military service, he devoted his life in a high-minded way to the best interests of the city as he saw them. The state requited him by executing him in his seventy-first year on charges of impiety and corrupting the young.

His extraordinary life is well-documented only in its later stages. Almost the only fact known about his youth is that he consorted with Archelaus, who introduced him to Ionian science. But after immersing himself for some time in this field of enquiry he decided he had no aptitude for such studies. Like the Sophists, with whom he was popularly identified, he began to devote all his attention to the study of man.

The long foreseen and long protracted war between Athens and Sparta broke out in 431, and during its opening decade Socrates served in the army as a hoplite, gaining a high reputation for courage in battle. By 423 he had become such a familiar figure in Athenian society that he could be given a leading role in the *Clouds* as an eccentric kind of intellectual running a 'thinking-shop'. This witty caricature at least indicates that he had already become the centre of a group of disciples, and there is independent evidence of this fact in the strange tale of his friend Chaerephon and the Delphic Oracle.

The story goes that Chaerephon asked the Oracle whether there was anyone wiser than Socrates, and the Oracle for once returned an unambiguous answer, saying No. Socrates took the incident seriously and so should we. It indicates that by middle age Socrates had already acquired a considerable reputation for 'wisdom', and this is best explained as arising from his encounters with visiting Sophists. All the great figures of the movement were in the habit of visiting Athens at this period, and it seems that Socrates used to take them on and defeat them at their own game of debate and argument. Such at least is the picture presented by Plato in his earlier dialogues, and there is no reason to doubt its general accuracy.

Socrates himself was not conscious of possessing any special wisdom, so he decided to test the meaning of the oracular response by questioning those Athenians who did claim to be more knowledgeable than the rest of the citizens. Those who submitted to his inquisition, and they included craftsmen, poets, and politicians, were easily shown up as muddled and opinionated in their views, and he soon satisfied himself that most, if not all, pretensions to superior knowledge were bogus. It then dawned on him that his own superiority as vouched for by the god lay in his honest admission of his own ignorance.

As one who sincerely claimed to know nothing he obviously could not set up as a teacher taking paying pupils, but a circle of disciples gathered round him because they admired his penetrating mind and found his conversation stimulating and improving. He in turn sought out the company of the young, frequenting the gymnasia where they would gather for athletic training, and engaging them in conversation when they were relaxing after exercise. The gymnasia were the informal schools and colleges of the time where the future leaders of society could be reached and influenced. Socrates thought that he could best serve the interests of Athens by getting these young aristocrats to think seriously about what he regarded as the most important of all questions, namely, 'How should a man lead his life?' Older men would join in such discussions too, and many who thought themselves good counsellors and prudent judges of affairs found their assumptions seriously tested, if not refuted, by the Socratic dialectic. They felt they had been humiliated in front of their juniors, and this contributed to the mounting store of suspicion and dislike which eventually brought Socrates to his death.

In 399, four years after the final defeat of Athens by Sparta, Socrates was brought to trial under an indictment which read as follows: 'Socrates does wrong, (1) in not respecting the gods which the city worships, and in introducing other new deities; (2) in corrupting the youth.' The prosecution was taken under the general rubric of 'impiety'. Athenian tolerance had come under increasing strain in the war years, and leading thinkers such as Anaxagoras and Protagoras had previously been prosecuted under the same statute. The charges were vague, but the political intention was clear. Socrates was deemed to be a subversive influence undermining the traditions and beliefs of Athenian society, and was to be silenced or driven into exile. He was suspected of oligarchic leanings because of the company he kept, and because he had criticised the rationale of election by lot, which was a central feature of the democratic system at Athens.

There were two widespread and deep-seated prejudices telling against him which could be traced back in part to his portrayal by the comic playwrights. He was supposed to be some kind of atheistic scientist (which he certainly was not), and he was known to have associated with two former opponents of the democracy, Alcibiades and Critias (though this did not prove he was himself in any way disloyal). This association was probably the main substance behind the charge of corrupting the youth, but in general the cautious and backward-looking politicians then in power disapproved of his habit of encouraging the young to think for themselves.

In the other scale he could only set his honesty of character, his high-minded desire to improve the moral tone of society, and his life-long loyalty to Athens. After a one-day trial, an absurdly short time for teasing out such complex issues, he was found guilty by the narrow margin of 260 to 240 votes. In the assessment of penalty which followed he refused to make a serious counter-proposal to offset the prosecution's demand for the death sentence, and was condemned by a larger majority for this characteristic piece of intransigence. He met his death with the same calm fortitude that he had shown in life. Thus perished one whom Plato called 'the best man of his time in wisdom and justice'.

What Socrates stood for

Socrates's pivotal position in the history of philosophy becomes clearer by comparison with the Sophists. He shared in their humanistic approach but was not interested in worldly success or political advancement. Like them, he was a firm believer in education, but he was also convinced that the only valid form of education is self-education. The Sophists wrote text-books, but he wrote nothing. He did not lay claim to have any special doctrines to impart, but he stood for a new and critical attitude to living.

His conception of philosophy is well expressed in some words which Plato puts into his mouth in the *Apology*:

> I shall never give up philosophising. I shall continue to give a clear exhortation to everyone I meet, using my customary language: 'My good Sir, you are an Athenian, a citizen of the city which is greatest and most noted for its wisdom and power. Are you not then ashamed to be worrying about your money and how to increase it, and about your reputation and your honour, instead of caring and worrying about the knowledge of good and truth and how to improve your soul?'

And if anyone retorts that he does so care, I shall not let him off at once and go away, but I shall question him, and examine him, and refute him.

This was his 'service to the god', his mission to the city arising from the Delphic Oracle, and not even the threat of death could deter him from it. He felt bound to make a sustained attempt to get people to realise their misconceptions and false beliefs about the most important things in life. Plato described him as a 'gadfly' whose function was to prick the lazy Athenian conscience into better action. In Socrates's opinion the true 'statesman' was one who made people 'better off' in the moral rather than the material sense. Socratic philosophising was a form of intellectual and moral confrontation, a sustained exhortation to care for the truth and improve the soul. Its method was conversational, and its first objective was the refutation of error. After that it could work to instill a true sense of values.

The Socratic method
The regular first move in a Socratic conversation was the exhortation 'Let us consider the problem together'. He got his hearers to tell him what they thought rather than telling them what to think. But the conversation was not allowed to become desultory. Socrates was a rigorous thinker, and insisted on a methodical approach to the ethical problems in which he was chiefly interested. The object of his enquiries was to establish an adequate understanding of commonly used moral terms such as courage, piety, friendship, and so on. His standard procedure was to induce some member of the company to say what he thought such terms meant. The statement was then treated as a provisional definition and subjected by Socrates to analysis and criticism.

Sometimes the analysis was simply designed to elucidate the meaning of the words used. But usually Socrates developed arguments to show that the provisional definition, or hypothesis, led to inconsistent or unacceptable consequences. The 'Socratic method' of question and answer was an important link in the chain of development that led to the emergence of the science of formal logic. The method was generally negative in outcome. It normally led to an *impasse* with no candidate hypotheses left in the field, and the company reduced to perplexity. Such a result was not unwelcome to Socrates, for he regarded it as the best way to disabuse people's minds of false opinions and prepare them for real insights. But it also led to Socrates getting an undeserved reputation as a sceptic, though he was really far removed from the Sophists in standing for the absolute validity of moral standards.

The ethical insights of Socrates

Our sources agree that Socrates was fond of drawing an analogy between art/skill and morality, and this formed part of the more positive side of his thought. He was impressed by the assured way in which various craftsmen went about their business, attributing this to the fact that each had a clear goal and an approved technique for achieving it. On this basis he seems to have argued inductively towards the conclusion that morality as the art/skill of living should also be capable of prescribing a clear goal (happiness or well-being) and a means of attaining it (right conduct). If morality is really a skill, it must involve 'know-how' and be based on knowledge. Socrates was always tending to suggest a close connection between the various virtues and intelligence. To be truly brave, or temperate, or just, one had to know what one was doing and why one was doing it. Being Socrates he did not spell this out dogmatically, but it seems to be implicit in his thinking as presented in the various dialogues and memoirs composed by his followers, including Xenophon and Plato.

The same sources indicate that he had worked out a scale of values with external goods (money and possessions) at the bottom, goods of the body (health and strength) somewhat higher up, and goods of the soul (moral integrity and moral insight) at the top. This scale was clearly reflected in his own conduct. Living frugally and ascetically, he despised wealth and luxury, and was capable of enduring poverty and hardship with equanimity. If you accept this scale of values, it follows that it is better to suffer injustice than to commit it. If you suffer it, you may lose your money, your freedom, even your life, but you retain your most valuable possession, your moral integrity. If you commit it, you may appear to have come off best in the transaction, but the worst damage is done to your own soul by the distortion and falsification of its moral perceptions. Convinced that the best way to promote self-betterment was through self-examination, he was fond of quoting the Delphic maxim, 'Know thyself', and one of his great sayings was: 'The unexamined life is not worth living.' In his company one was continually challenged to 'tendance of the soul'.

This brings us to the central core of Socratic ethics, which is usually summed up in the twin paradoxes: 'no one does wrong willingly', and 'virtue is knowledge'. Socrates may have said the first, but the second probably represents Plato's summary of his message. Together the maxims underline the optimism and the rationalism of Socrates's outlook. He belonged to the 'great genera-tion' of Protagoras and Pericles, and shared their confidence in the general good sense of ordinary people. If people acted immorally, that must, he thought, be due to ignorance rather than perversity.

Clearly, if virtue is knowledge, vice must be ignorance. In what does the ignorance consist? Socrates analysed it as ignorance of the true nature of 'good', that is to say, of what is ultimately desirable or beneficial for the individual. This is where his scale of goods comes in. If one accepts that goods of the soul are best, one is on the way to accepting the Virtue=Knowledge paradox. Socrates was convinced that in the last analysis the 'virtue' or 'excellence' of a human being depends on his soul's possession of 'knowledge', by which he meant 'rational insight' into the principles of conduct. He believed that if such insight were achieved the person would inevitably do what was right and good both for himself and for others.

If it was objected that people often know what they ought to do, but fail to do it, Socrates would reply that such people are weak-willed, and have not acquired the strength of real knowledge. In his view, to be weak-willed is not to have a will at all, because one cannot 'will', though one may desire, what is bad for one. In such a case, he thought, the desire is grounded in opinion rather than knowledge. Hence his determination to expose sham or counterfeit 'knowledge'.

The essence of Socratic ethics may be summed up as follows: knowledge in the sense of insight into spiritual values is a rare possession. True willing means consciously desiring what is ulti-mately and absolutely good, namely, goodness of 'soul', 'mind' or 'personality'. To go wrong, or do wrong, is to close one's eyes to the truth that misconduct results in harm to oneself, and no one in his view can truly will such an outcome. The circle of argument is closed by the practical reflection that the best and surest way to improve one's conduct is to acquire the kind of self-knowledge or 'insight' which will inevitably result in good living. Such knowledge will unify and integrate the personality, so the unity of virtue follows from his principles as well as its equation with knowledge. And since true knowledge is insight, there is a paramount need and duty to 'tend one's soul'.

Nowadays a command to 'tend the soul' would be regarded as a religious rather than a moral exhortation, and there is, I think, no doubt that Socrates was a deeply religious man. Plato, who knew him very well, represents him as praying to the god Pan and composing a hymn to Apollo, and records his last words prescribing a sacrifice to Asklepios the god of healing. Socrates was the least hypocritical of men, so we must suppose that he thought it right to use the conventional avenues of the time for access to spiritual reality. He had a very high conception of the nature of deity, and so, like Xenophanes, he was critical of the fact that Greek mythology often depicted the gods in a very immoral light. Such criticism could be misrepresented as an attack on religion itself, and this certainly told against him at his trial. He also used to speak of his 'divine sign' which from time to time used to come to him like an inner voice warning him to refrain from certain actions. The malicious gossip of Athens probably represented this as some kind of illicit private oracle, and it doubtless underlies the charge that he 'introduced new deities'. Like many another martyr he was spiritually in advance of his time. Because of his emphasis on the guiding light of conscience he has been well called the first nonconformist in history.

Socrates's position in the history of thought
Socrates's crucial role in the development of Greek philosophy is underlined by the term 'Presocratic'. All the thinkers before him, and some of those contemporary with him, are classified as Presocratics because in their various ways they were all trying to comprehend the ultimate nature of the Universe. Socrates marks a definitive shift in emphasis away from philosophy as the study of nature and towards philosophy as a 'way of life'. This was not a one-man revolution. Socrates was part and parcel of the general humanistic trend also exemplified by the Sophists. But the influence of the Sophists was diffused throughout the whole of the educational system, whereas the influence of Socrates was highly concentrated in his inner circle of friends and followers. They taught, but he provided inspiration.

92

Socrates was largely responsible for making the problem of conduct the central issue in Greek thought, and after him ethics always retained a dominant position in the various philosophical schools. In the next generation the most influential thinkers were all 'Socratics' in that they took up and emphasised various aspects of Socrates's outlook and way of life. From Socrates on, a new note makes itself heard in the history of ethics and education: the note of the importance of the inner life, of spiritual culture. Socrates's unworldly attitude was carried over into the Cynic School, into Platonism, into Stoic thought, and ultimately fused with the message of Christianity. 'What shall it profit a man if he gain the whole world and lose his soul?' is a very Socratic question. After the sack of Megara the victorious general asked Stilpo the Socratic to send in an account of the goods he had lost, and Stilpo replied: 'No one looted my inner resources.' All this is not to say that science was subsequently neglected — far from it. Mathematics and astronomy continued to make great strides, particularly in Plato's Academy, and later in Alexandria. But a gap now tended to open up between the scientists and the Socratics. Plato wanted to bridge this gap, and tried to do so along Pythagorean lines, but he must also be regarded as a Socratic because of his devoted and effective propagation of the memory, methods, and ideals of Socrates.

8

IDEALISM AND EDUCATION: PLATO AND THE ACADEMY

PLATO (427–347) was an aristocratic Athenian, descended on his father's side from one of the early kings of Athens, and on his mother's from the famous statesman Solon. Socrates was a friend of his close relatives Critias and Charmides, and Plato must have known him from boyhood on, and must have been often in his company during the last decade of the fifth century. From 409 on Plato would have been liable for military duties, and he probably served with the cavalry in the closing years of the war against Sparta. In 404/3 he was invited to join in the oligarchic rule of the 'thirty tyrants' (who included Critias and Charmides), but the junta fell from power while he hesitated. Four years later he was appalled and disgusted by the execution of Socrates under the restored democracy. One party appeared as bad as the other, and Athenian politics seemed to hold no future for him.

For the next twelve years or so he indulged in authorship and desultory travel, and in *c.*387, when he had turned forty, he set out on a trip to western Greece. His first port of call was Taras (Taranto), where he made friends with a remarkable man called Archytas. Archytas was a successful general and statesman, and also a mathematician of genius. Significantly too he was a member of the Pythagorean Order. He must have seemed to Plato to be a living embodiment of his ideal concept of the philosopher-king.

From Taras he voyaged on to the large and opulent city of Syracuse which was then under the rule of the ruthlessly successful autocrat Dionysius I. There he met a young nobleman called Dion, who carried much influence at court, and he and Plato struck up a warm friendship. Plato's homosexual tendency is evident in this event. There can be little doubt that he fell passionately in love with Dion. Indeed he tells us as much in the last line of one of his elegant verse epigrams: 'O Dion, you who maddened my heart with love.' Plato's view of such a love is made clear in the *Phaedrus*, where he says that if pursued in a restrained and honourable spirit it has the power to educate and elevate the souls of both partners. This, and not timid admiration from a safe distance, is Plato's own conception of 'Platonic love'.

The role of love as an educational force is a major theme in Plato's thought. He accepted that sexual attraction is the basis and beginning of love, and that the segregation of the sexes (very marked in Athenian society), and the role of the gymnasium in education, would make it likely that adult males would be attracted to boys. It is easy to be flippant or cynical about such attachments, but Plato refused to depreciate them. He wanted to see them forming the basis of ennobling friendships, and the partnerships used as a means of progress in philosophical understanding.

In the Seventh of the Letters preserved in the Platonic corpus (which I accept as genuine), Plato claims that by appropriately Socratic exhortation he was able to wean Dion away from habits of luxury and self-indulgence towards a more sober and 'philosophic' way of life. They continued to keep in touch after Plato's return to Athens, and their friendship was to have momentous consequences for the future political development of Syracuse.

Plato's life-work now took definite shape as a direct result of this first visit to Sicily. As I interpret it, he underwent something like a 'conversion' experience. In the classic pattern of such experiences a time of frustration and self-doubt is suddenly followed, after a heightening emotional stimulus, by a period when the individual is filled with a sense of mission and purpose. Plato's long-standing uncertainty about how to contribute to Athenian public life now fell away, and was replaced by a clear-eyed vision of what he was best fitted to do. Seeing the effect that his words had on Dion he realised that the mantle of Socrates had fallen on his shoulders, and that he was destined to become a moral guide to the youth of Greece. At the same time he still wanted to make some political contribution, and the example of Archytas and the Pythagorean Order showed him that philosophical studies were not inconsistent with political influence. If he could not enter politics himself he would make his ideas felt through his pupils.

All these considerations now came together in his mind, and resulted in the decision to found in Athens a permanent teaching institution, the Academy, which was destined to become the proto-type of all subsequent colleges and universities. The Academy took its name from a dead and semi-deified Attic hero, Academus, who was worshipped in a pleasant wooded area some little distance to the north-west of the city. Plato acquired a property there, including a gymnasium, and opened a school designed as a philosophical sem-inary for the training of a new type of leader for the Greek world. The buildings included lecture rooms, residences, and a common dining hall. Plato was the first head of the school, which attracted what would now be called research fellows as well as younger students.

The institution as a whole was organised as a cult-group, the ancient equivalent in law of a corporate body, and this enabled the property to be vested in the members of the school, and transmitted down the centuries for the continuance of the founder's intentions. The stated object of the cult was appropriate — the worship of the Muses. The actual date of the foundation is not known for certain — it must have been about 386 or 385 — and the tradition is that the school lasted until its official closure under the Byzantine emperor Justinian in AD529. This would give it a longer life span than any similar modern institution has yet achieved with the sole exception of the al-Azhar in Cairo.

Plato's purpose in founding the Academy was practical and statesmanlike. He wanted to provide a more rigorous and princi-pled alternative to sophistic or rhetorical training, and there is plenty of evidence that many of his pupils did go out to provide enlightened and effective leadership in their city-states. They were particularly in demand as advisers in constitution-making or the drafting of new legislation.

For the next twenty years or so he was fully occupied in devel-oping the Academy and composing a number of major dialogues, including his *magnum opus* the *Republic*. This work of genius centres round the paradox of the 'philosopher-king', and in effect constitutes a prospectus for the new school.

In 367 Dionysius I died, and Dion invited Plato back to Syracuse to act as adviser to his successor Dionysius II. Dion hoped that Plato would exert a good influence over the new ruler, but Plato was reluctant to leave Athens on what he suspected would be a rather forlorn enterprise. When he arrived in Syracuse his worst fears were confirmed. The new ruler was a feeble character politically and intellectually, and Plato could make no headway with his education. He also had to contend with an anti-Dion faction which suspected, perhaps not without reason, that Dion was plotting to seize power for himself. In the event Dion was soon driven into exile, and Plato returned to Athens with very little to show for his visit.

He made one further visit to Sicily in 362–361, but the sad saga of unrest there continued. In 357 Dion resorted to force, capturing Syracuse with a band of mercenaries, and expelling Dionysius. He ruled for three years until treacherously murdered by one of his own subordinates. Plato then wrote his Seventh Letter to the remnants of Dion's party, but peace did not return to the city until some years after his own death. This was in 347. He was intellectually productive to the end, and died 'pen in hand', working on a revision of his last and longest dialogue, the *Laws*.

Writings

All that Plato wrote and published is still extant. His authorship extended over about fifty years, and during this long period he produced a constant stream of works of great variety and charm, as well as high philosophic importance.

The separate works, numbering more than thirty, have not come down to us with dates of publication, and their chronological order has been the subject of prolonged debate. Using the *Laws* as a final fixed point of reference, stylometric analysis has demonstrated that the dialogues divide into an 'early', a 'middle', and a 'late' group, but the method is not sufficiently precise to establish the exact ordering within each group.

The 'early' group comprises the *Apology* and *Crito* and all the shorter dialogues, in which the definitions of various virtues are canvassed inconclusively. It also includes the longer and brilliantly dramatic *Protagoras* and *Gorgias*. The main object of the dialogues of this group is to pay tribute to Socrates and to immortalise his memory. They may plausibly be assigned to the twelve years between Socrates's death (399) and the first Sicilian visit (*c.*387).

The 'middle' group centres round Plato's single most important work, the *Republic*. Socrates is still a dominant figure, but more Platonic features now begin to appear, notably an interest in

Pythagoreanism. The group includes some of the best loved dialogues, like *Phaedo* and *Symposium*, which may be taken to precede the *Republic*. After the *Republic* come more strictly philosophical works, like the *Parmenides* and the *Theaetetus* (datable to *c.*369). The group as a whole is to be dated to the period between the first and second Sicilian visits (*c.* 387 and 367). It clearly reflects Plato's growing involvement with the work of the Academy, together with the development of his own philosophy from its Socratic roots.

There is general agreement that the 'late' group comprises *Sophist*, *Statesman*, *Philebus*, *Timaeus*, *Critias* and *Laws*, very possibly in that order, a remarkable output for a man in his late sixties and seventies. A measurable stylistic difference between the last works of the middle group and the opening works of this group suggests that there was a gap in Platonic authorship during the years of his closest involvement with Sicilian affairs, 367–362. If this is correct he will then have resumed creative writing on his return from the West in 360. The late group represents his output from then until his death in 347.

Nearly all of these works are cast in dialogue form, and the named characters who appear in them are real historical individuals. This fact, combined with the fact that Plato himself does not overtly appear (though his *persona* is only thinly concealed by un-named 'strangers' in the *Sophist* and the *Laws*), raises the question of how far the dialogues convey Plato's own thought. The problem is particularly acute when, as often, Socrates is the main speaker.

I believe that a reasonable solution is possible without going to the extreme of attributing too much to Socrates, or despairing of ever getting at Plato's own philosophy. Broadly speaking I would maintain that the 'early' dialogues are thoroughly Socratic in their concentration on ethical topics, but that even here Plato's system-building mind is already at work imposing general formulae like 'Virtue is Knowledge' on the more loosely structured and pragmatic scheme of values espoused by Socrates. In the 'middle' dialogues Socrates is still given prominence as a leader of discussion, but he is tending more and more to become a mere mouthpiece for Plato, especially when the theory of Forms is being expounded. In the 'late' works Socrates rarely even appears, and the thought is entirely Platonic.

Thought: the theory of Forms

Plato confronted the scepticism of his time with an unwavering belief in the possibility of real knowledge. Two conditions, he thought, must be satisfied for knowledge to occur: the object of knowledge must be an unchanging object, and it must be directly grasped by the mind. As a young man he became friendly with a follower of Heraclitus called Cratylus, who convinced him that all sensible objects are impermanent things in a continual state of flux. As such, they could be perceived but not known. He had, then, to look for non-sensible objects of a permanent nature which would be accessible to the knowing mind, and he found significant examples of such objects in the virtues and values which Socrates was trying to define and defend.

To Plato's mind nothing could be more real and more important than ideal beauty and absolute goodness. Such objects became for him the focus of knowledge and the substance of permanently valid truth. He saw in them the great controlling patterns that lie behind the changing face of the visible world, and he called such patterns 'Ideas', adopting as part of his terminology the Greek word *idea** which basically means 'form' (and has nothing in common with the English 'idea'). I shall follow the convention of using capital letters for Idea/Form since it is a useful way of emphasising the unique and objective nature of these objects. A Platonic Form (Idea) is not a thought in someone's mind but something that exists *per se* as an immutable part of the structure of reality.

Ethical Forms were not the only ideal patterns that he recognised. He also drew strong support for his theory from Pythagorean doctrine with its emphasis on number as the formative element and underlying substance of things. Plato would have agreed with the statement that water is really H_2O. The Form can be readily understood as a *formula* provided one allows it an existence independent of the thinking mind. An empirical thinker might argue that a formula like H_2O is an abstraction and less real than a drop of water, but Plato was no empiricist. On the contrary, he was the most influential idealist in the history of philosophy. Nothing could shake his conviction that the relationship expressed by a formula like 'equal to two right angles' is more real (because more permanent) than any particular triangle. His whole philosophical career was devoted to drawing out the implications of this fundamental intuition.

Plato's world of Forms, then, is constituted by ideal objects or patterns, such as Beauty, Equality, Circularity, Health, and Justice. The Forms are invisible and intangible, and can only be apprehended by the mind after suitable preparation and training. They exist eternally, with a transcendent nature that sets them apart from our world, but by a process of 'creation' (for which see below, pp.107–8), the visible world has been modelled after them, and their essential qualities are diffused down into the particular things that we touch and see. When we exclaim at the beauty of a face or comment on the justice of a decision, we are, in Plato's view, generalising our experiences and rendering them intelligible in the light of the Forms that we have glimpsed inhering in them. Beautiful things, he says, become beautiful by the presence in them of Beauty, and the same is true of just things. In general, the presence of a Form is the cause of the qualities that characterise particular objects.

Two important subsidiary doctrines buttress the central arch of the theory of Forms: (1) that Opinion is entirely distinct from Knowledge; (2) that there are Degrees of Reality.

(1) Opinion, unlike Knowledge, is variable because it is derived from the changing phenomena of the everyday world. Opinions are formed on the basis of sense perception, and are flawed by contradictions and illusions. People can be made to change their opinions by irrational pressures, and even if opinions are correct they can only be affirmed not proved. Knowledge, by contrast, is the end-product of reasoning. It can be proved and demonstrated, and is held firm by the proof. Opinions are often false, but 'false knowledge' is a contradiction in terms. Knowledge does not rest in any way on sense perception, but is a function of the mind making direct contact with the Forms.

According to doctrine (2), reality is concentrated in the invisible world of Forms, which are *more real* than the fleeting and insubstantial particulars in the visible world. But particulars are not viewed as totally unreal. They share to some extent in reality in so far as Forms are present in them. There are degrees of reality also within the visible world, with shadows and reflections rating as less real than solid objects like plants and animals. By analogy the upper World contains 'mathematical' objects like perfect circles, which are less real than the Form of Circularity which they reflect.

The Forms were so crucial and central in Plato's philosophy that he was reluctant to disclose all his thinking about them in what he regarded as the inadequate and inferior medium of the written word. The evidence of Aristotle makes it clear that within the Academy there was much discussion of the more abstruse aspects of the theory. It seems certain that Plato held well-articulated views about the theoretical basis of mathematics, and about the relation of Forms to Numbers, none of which he published in his dialogues. These were the so-called 'unwritten doctrines' which I shall not attempt to discuss in this necessarily summary sketch of Platonism. They were certainly difficult and esoteric, but not in principle incommunicable. Plato, I believe, lectured about them to his pupils; they were known in detail to Aristotle and others; and the painstaking work of modern scholars has recovered their main outlines. It would be wrong to suppose that Plato had one set of doctrines for the general public and quite another set for his intimates. Plato's thought formed a unity, but only some of it was expressed in the dialogues. One might compare it to a mountain range whose highest peak remains veiled in the clouds though the approximate height and location of the summit can be inferred from the lower contours.

One may reasonably suppose that the apex of Plato's thought was reached in his account of the Form of the Good. Aristotle says that he used to lecture on the nature of the Good, puzzling many of his hearers because they expected an ethical rather than a metaphysical treatment. In the dialogues little or nothing is said directly about the Good beyond one rather veiled reference to its manifestation in the triple guise of 'beauty, symmetry, and truth'. But at the end of Book VI of the *Republic* its status in relation to the world of Forms is significantly compared to the status of the sun in relation to the world we inhabit. This is Plato's way of emphasising its transcendent power and significance.

The details of the comparison are significant. Just as sunlight enables us to gain a clear and distinct view of the objects surrounding us in the visible world, so the Form of the Good renders all lesser Forms meaningful and intelligible. The rays of truth emanating from it are the medium in which all other objects of the mind are to be viewed and known. But the sun stands in an even more vital and creative role in relation to our planet as the ultimate source of its energy and existence. In the same way the Form of the Good, Plato suggests, is the creative and sustaining power from which the other

Forms derive their very being. It is the ultimate One over the many, transcending even reality itself in authority and power.

Plato's view of justice: state and individual in the *Republic*

One of Plato's main aims was to demonstrate against the Sophists that the state has a natural and not just a conventional basis. He found its origins in fundamental human needs or wants, such as food and shelter, which cause human beings to associate together for mutual protection and help. In such associations the principle of division of labour is at once seen to be beneficial, as well as being in accordance with natural differences of talent. Those who have 'green fingers' take to growing food for the whole community, those with constructional ability build houses, and those with craft skills make clothes and shoes. The smallest possible 'city', as he memorably put it, consists of a farmer, a builder, a weaver, a shoe-maker, and one other (possibly a carpenter!). But such an embryonic community will hardly be viable for long, and the city soon expands to encompass other skilled craftsmen, and as it grows in wealth acquires shop-keepers and merchants.

Its wealth makes it a possible target for aggressive neighbours, and the problem of providing security takes the argument on to a new stage. The principle of 'one man, one job' must be followed, and a special class of 'guardians' must be created and trained to be the professional defenders of the state. This is achieved by the early selection of talented children, who are then put through a 'grammar-school' type of education, distinct from the vocational training of craft apprentices. When the 'guardians' reach the age of eighteen they are further tested to find those with a real aptitude for ruling, and only a small élite group is allowed to proceed to 'third-level' studies. After a long and arduous course including geometry, astronomy, and a 'dialectical' training in philosophy, they emerge as 'ruler-guardians'. The others settle down as 'helper-guardians', assisting the rulers in a military and executive capacity.

I have omitted a wealth of detail to give this very brief outline of Plato's ideal state. It consists of three distinct classes, each with a distinct function. The largest class, whom we may call the 'producers', are responsible for running the economy, and have no share in government. Above them stands the class of 'helper-guardians' who are responsible for defence and security. They are answerable to the top class of 'ruler-guardians', who are in fact 'philosopher-kings', trained to possess an insight into the nature of goodness and justice, and totally altruistic in their desire to translate this knowledge into sound legislation and effective policy-making for the benefit of the whole state. The totalitarian bias of the pattern is clear, but there are some liberal features in the scheme, notably Plato's insistence that women must receive the same education as men and be equally eligible for supreme power.

Plato hints that it will be difficult, perhaps impossible, to realise this pattern in an actual state. The ideal state stands as an ideal limit at which reform should aim. It also has an important role in the ethical argument of the *Republic*, providing a large-scale model of the human personality and how it should function.

Plato regards it as axiomatic that the three classes reflect three 'parts' in the 'soul'. 'Soul' in this context means 'character' or 'personality', and 'part' is best understood as 'motivation' or 'tendency'. Plato thinks that there are three main tendencies or 'drives' which activate human nature, the acquisitive, the combative, and the intellectual.

At the base of the human personality lies a disorderly mass of instincts and desires which he calls the 'appetitive element'. Above and distinct from this lower part of our nature is the 'spirited element'. It is the part of us which feels anger and resentment, and where ambition and self-respect are principally located. The highest part of our soul is called the 'rational element', yet another instance of Plato's tendency to equate mind and soul. The existence of the different parts is proved by the conflict of motives which we so often experience. An obvious example would be the desire for alcohol conflicting with rational considerations and thus highlighting polar extremes in the personality. The separate identity of the spirited element is more subtly shown by the case of one who is 'angry with himself' for giving in to a morbid craving. Here the anger is directed against the desire and so must be distinct from it.

Plato is not advocating total supression of desire. Desires for food, drink, and sex have a part to play in ensuring individual and group survival. His point is that they must operate under the control of the upper elements if the personality is to function as a harmonious and well-integrated unity. The function of the rational element is to plan and coordinate all our activities in our best long-term interests. On its own it may lack the power to overcome a strong desire, and this is where the function of the spirited element comes in. This element has a natural tendency to side with reason, cherishing self-respect and chiding lapses, and it thus reinforces the dictates of reason and makes them effective.

This psychological doctrine enables Plato to give a coherent account of the four chief virtues of traditional Greek ethics. Wisdom is the virtue of the rational element in control of the personality and consciously directing its activities towards good goals. Courage is the virtue of the spirited element lending strength and purpose to the intellect, and so preserving intact the scheme of values and the standards of behaviour that have been inculcated by the educational system. Temperance (that is, self-control) is given a more subtle analysis. It is not just the subjection of lower to higher nature, nor is it fully realised when there is tension and conflict between the elements. Temperance at its best is a condition of inner harmony, with reason consenting to rule and the desires consenting to operate under its authority. Justice, finally, turns out to have been foreshadowed in the basic principle of 'one man, one job'. A man, like a community, is just if the various elements in his nature are able to fulfil their proper functions without intruding on the functions of another part. This is only possible under the 'rule of reason'. If the other elements attempt to usurp power the personality becomes distorted and corrupted, and in a word unjust.

Plato's *Republic* is a magnificent handbook of moral philosophy. In the spirit of Socrates he internalises morality and relates it to self-knowledge and self-control, but he also manages to integrate it into the structure of society. The nature of the virtues is identical in the state and the individual. A just man and a just society exhibit the same pattern of parts functioning harmoniously in an ordered whole. With the aid of a sound psychological analysis Plato pays due attention to the importance of education in character development. His theory of Forms provides a framework that gives meaning and purpose to man's noblest aspirations, and integrates them into the structure of the cosmos.

Plato on the soul: reincarnation and recollection
It is clear from the dialogues that Plato believed in the pre-existence of the soul, as well as in its continued existence after death. He fully accepted the Pythagorean doctrine of reincarnation (see above, pp.34–5), and added a new philosophical dimension to it with his own theory of recollection.

According to this theory the soul in some previous dis-carnate state has been able to journey through the heavens in direct contemplation of the eternal Forms. The shock of falling down to earth to be born in human shape causes a temporary forgetfulness of this vision, but memory traces remain in the mind and can be re-awakened by suitable analysis and questioning of the data of experience. For example, one can look at pairs of sticks or stones and judge that they are nearly, but not quite, equal. Since we have never had experience of absolute equality in this life, Plato asks how such judgements are possible. And he answers that latent memories of the relevant Forms are being elicited through experience of the particular things in which they are imperfectly exemplified. Just as we cannot judge a portrait as a likeness unless we have had prior acquaintance with the person depicted, so, he argues, our judgements about the inadequacies of sensible things must rest on a prior knowledge of the Forms in their full perfection. And since we cannot achieve the fullness of such knowledge while in the body, it follows that the contemplative experience must have occurred before birth. As Wordsworth puts it: 'Our birth is but a sleep and a forgetting...'; and as Plato sums it up in a striking phrase: 'Learning is recollecting.'

In the learning process we classify and order the raw data of sensation with the aid of general concepts. Plato interprets this process as an ascent of the mind/soul from the level of the particular to a higher level of generality in which the particular is seen in a derivative relationship with a Form or Forms. This ladder of ascent is explicitly described in a notable passage of the *Symposium* where the soul in quest of beauty is said to rise from admiration of one or two beautiful bodies to the contemplation of all beautiful bodies, and from thence to a study of noble character, and from thence to a grasp of the elegances of science, until finally the quest culminates in knowledge of the essence of beauty itself. The process has obvious analogies with forms of ecstatic experience in which the rapt soul is said to enjoy a 'mystical union' with the Godhead. When Plato's philosophising is infused with emotional warmth it turns into a form of theology.

In the *Phaedrus* he pictures the immortal soul as a kind of fallen angel which loses its wings when it is thrust down into a mortal body. If it then responds to spiritual influences — and the experience of beauty is a potent vehicle for such influences — it will succeed in growing its wings again, and when released from the body after death may succeed in regaining its former state of bliss. Permanent release from the cycle of reincarnation is the ultimate reward of the soul that has been purified and enlightened by philosophical contemplation. Plato has here transposed into a philosophic key certain doctrines of the Greek mystery cults in which the initiate was promised that after death he would either be with the gods or become a god. To Plato's mind the true interpretation of the soul's immortality is to affirm that it has the possibility of sharing fully in divine life. If it neglects its opportunities by failing to respond to moral or intellectual stimulus it will sink down in the scale of being, and if it wilfully chooses vicious or evil conduct it will receive appropriate punishment in the after-life.

Plato's philosophical method: dialectic

So far I have tended to emphasise the intuitive element in Plato's conception of knowledge. But he recognised also that the road to knowledge has to be systematically paved with a progressive understanding of propositions and their relationships. The philosopher must be able to give an account of what he claims to know, and he does this through dialectic.

In Hegel and Marx the term 'dialectic', which was perhaps coined by Plato, has moved a long way from its basic meaning of 'the art of discussion'. Dialectic (*dialektike**) originated as a disciplined way of asking and answering questions about reality. In developing its methods and prescribing its objectives Plato owed something to Zeno but much more to the group discussions held by Socrates. Its objective was to gain a systematic understanding of the Forms, and it was regarded by Plato as the 'coping-stone' of the sciences. In his day the leading sciences were arithmetic, geometry, astronomy, and harmonics. He gave these disciplines an honoured place in his system of higher education because they encouraged abstract ways of thought, and so trained the mind to look beyond the surface appearance of things. But he regarded them as essentially preparatory to the philosopher's main endeavour. They could not bring the thinker to the fullness of truth because they still relied to some extent on sense perception and sensible data. Also, they operated with untested axioms and definitions as their starting-points, a feature particularly evident in the case of geometry.

The true nature of Plato's dialectic emerges in the light of these criticisms. It was scientific philosophising, and could only be fruitfully undertaken by a mind that had been thoroughly schooled in purely abstract thinking. It had to operate entirely in the world of Forms, without making any use of sense data or relying on any untested starting-point. As described in the *Republic* the method is essentially hypothetical and anti-dogmatic. Propositions must be formulated, but no proposition is to be taken as sacrosanct. All are to be subject to scrutiny. Dialectic must be thoroughgoing in its programme of testing every intellectual starting-point.

This road of enquiry leads 'upward' in the sense that it proceeds to establish ever wider generalisations that express the essence of ever more comprehensive Forms. Ultimately, in Plato's view, there must be one highest Form that comprehends all lower Forms, and when the hypothesising of dialectic reaches this point it can go no higher, because no wider generalisation is possible. In Plato's terminology, it has reached the 'unhypothetical first beginning'. This is the goal of dialectic. The mind of the enquirer is now able to envisage and grasp with an intuitive certainty the Form of Unity, which is the same as the Form of the Good.

Plato's cosmology

Plato totally rejected the Atomists' view of the universe as an indefinite plurality of chance-caused worlds. Instead he elaborated a theory which made divine mind the primal cause of the natural world, and put spiritual values at the heart of creation. The heavens, in his view, declare the rational purposes of their Maker, whose handiwork constitutes a 'cosmos', a single, ordered, and beautiful whole, infused with life and intelligence. Plato's world is an organic unity whose parts are intelligible by virtue of their mathematical structure.

The details of his scheme are chiefly given in the *Timaeus*, where the main speaker is a Pythagorean. Plato owed a major debt to Pythagorean advances in astronomy and mathematics, which he synthesised into a scheme that also embodied the four traditional elements of Fire, Air, Water, and Earth. The basic features of his scheme are a Maker and a Model. The Model consists of eternal and invisible Forms, and the visible and tangible world that the Maker brought, and brings, into existence reflects the goodness and beauty of their unseen but intelligible reality. The mysterious transcendence of the Maker is emphasised when Timaeus declares at the outset: 'It is hard to discover the Maker and Father of this universe, and even if one found Him it would be impossible to speak of Him to all.' His existence and activity are assumed as a necessary pre-condition of scientific explanation, but His nature is not elaborated as an object of worship.

The Maker's work resembles and reproduces the Model as far as possible, but like a human craftsman He has to work with somewhat intractable materials. His work has to be extended in a Space that is given not made, and has to incorporate a material substratum subject to random and disorderly motion. There is an element of 'brute fact' in the created world that resists the imposition of order and is not totally predictable in its movements.

Within these limits the Maker creates the World on the pattern of the Form of Life. This Form exists in eternal perfection and total independence from the Maker. Part of the pattern consists of Soul conjoined with Body, and this feature is reflected in the created cosmos. There is a World Soul which is the cause of regular motion, and the World's Body consists of four primary bodies, Fire, Air, Water, and Earth, which exist in strictly limited quantities indissolubly bonded together by the geometrical proportion obtaining between their volumes. The World Body is spherical in shape, not subject to any decay or dissolution, and revolves perpetually on its axis. There is no void either within or outside it, and no surrounding reservoir of material from which it replenishes itself. The World Soul is inserted into the centre of the sphere and permeates it throughout, endowing it with motion, life, and thought. Both Body and Soul are essential features of the World, but Soul is the senior partner because of its superior lineage. This World is such a self-sufficient and noble entity that it must be regarded as a god who has come into existence, planned and fashioned by the eternal Maker. The heavenly bodies including the planets are formed as part of its divine structure, and in their motions serve to mark the passage of Time, which Plato describes as a 'moving image of eternity'. The task of creating human beings is delegated to the lesser gods both visible (that is, Earth and the celestial bodies) and invisible (Zeus and the other gods of Greek tradition) who have now been brought into existence.

One of the most significant features of the whole complex scheme is the account of the structure of the primary elemental bodies of Fire, Air, Water, and Earth. Their corpuscular structure is related to the shapes of the regular solids. Fire is analysed into tetrahedra (four-sided shapes), earth into cubes (six-sided), air into octahedra (eight-sided), and water into icosahedra (twenty-sided). These shapes can be further analysed into component triangles of two kinds which Greek mathematicians called 'half-square' and 'half-triangle' because the former was produced by bisecting a square diagonally, and the latter by taking an equilateral triangle and dropping a perpendicular from one angle on to the opposite side. The former construction produces a right-angled isosceles triangle whose angles are in the proportion 1:1:2; the latter a right-angled scalene triangle whose angles are in the proportion 1:2:3. This gives a mathematical account of the elements of matter which is recognisably modern in spirit even though the details would no longer be scientifically acceptable.

The account allows for the transformation of one element into another by the decomposition of their structural shapes into basic triangles which can then be re-formed to give different solids. Plato is in fact rejecting the notion of a single fundamental type of *matter* underlying change. When air, for example, is condensed into water, the change, in his view, is not due to a greater concentration of material substance, but rather to an internal alteration of structure. A permanent substratum or framework in which such alterations can occur is provided by the notion of Space, which is a third basic factor in Plato's scheme of creation, quite distinct from intelligible Being on the one hand and perceptible Becoming on the other.

Epilogue

A quotation from Aristotle's memorial tribute will serve to round off my account of Plato. 'By his mode of life', said his greatest pupil, 'and by his method of philosophising, he set before mankind the clear conclusion that the quest for happiness is the same as the quest for excellence.' Plato is still the prince of moral philosophers. At the highest pitch of their inspiration his dialogues enshrine the record of a passionate pilgrimage on the road to goodness and truth. Stylist and sage, eloquent exponent of eternal values, the fountain-head of idealism, his thought still beats strongly at the heart of philosophical enquiry, commanding the affection and respect of all true lovers of wisdom.

9

SYSTEM AND SCIENCE: ARISTOTLE AND THE LYCEUM

ARISTOTLE (384–322) was a native of Stagira, an obscure little city in eastern Macedonia originally colonised by Ionians. His family was a wealthy one, and his father Nicomachus (who died when he was quite young) held the post of physician to Amyntas, the king of Macedonia. His father's profession helps to account for his special interest in biology, and the connection with the Macedonian court brought Aristotle into contact with the dynasty that was destined to dominate Greece and transform world history.

At the age of seventeen he went to Athens to study at the Academy, and resided there as a school member for twenty years. Plato showed his appreciation of Aristotle's intellectual powers by nicknaming him 'The Brain'. Aristotle in turn was probably not without some influence on his teacher, and the close-knit argumentation of some of Plato's later dialogues may well owe something to Aristotle's logical acumen. He always retained a deep respect for Plato as a man, even though he came to criticise and reject the theory of Forms. The effort which that rejection cost him is reflected in his moving remark: 'Friends and truth are both dear, but it is a sacred duty to prefer the truth.'

After the death of Plato in 347 Aristotle left Athens, and resided for time in Assos and then in Lesbos, where he conducted zoological research. In 343 Philip II invited him back to Pella to become tutor to his son Alexander, then a youth of fourteen. He compiled manuals for his young pupil on *Monarchy* and *Colonists*, and to judge from Alexander's later career this part of his tuition at least would seem to have had a considerable effect. So Socrates taught Plato, and Plato taught Aristotle, and Aristotle taught Alexander the Great, undoubtedly the most famous names ever to be linked in such a relationship.

The tuition lasted until Alexander's appointment as regent in 340. Alexander did not forget his tutor, if we may accept the story that he later gave a large endowment to his new school. This was the celebrated institution known as the Lyceum which Aristotle started in Athens in 335, soon after Alexander's accession to the Macedonian throne.

Like the Academy, the Lyceum occupied a gymnasium site some distance outside the city walls, but in a north-easterly direction. It took its name from 'Lyceius', a cult title of Apollo, who was worshipped in a sacred grove nearby. Its members came to be called 'Peripatetics' after the *Peripatos* (colonnaded courtyard) which formed part of the school's buildings, and where Aristotle was said to have strolled up and down while conducting lectures and discussions. In its organisation the Lyceum patterned itself on the Academy, but from the start it seems to have had more of the flavour of a research institute. Aristotle stressed the need to form collections of material as a basis for systematic study of any kind, and the Lyceum collections included manuscripts, maps, and zoological specimens. Alexander is said to have helped this aspect of the work by ordering fishermen and hunters throughout his empire to send in any rare specimens captured. The history of the school can be traced down to the second century AD.

Aristotle remained head of the Lyceum for thirteen years. After losing his wife Pythias he lived with Herpyllis from Stagira, who bore him a son called Nicomachus. He died in 322 at Chalcis (home of his mother's family), having been forced to leave Athens by an outburst of anti-Macedonian feeling after the death of Alexander in 323. As Aristotle wittily said, he retired in case the Athenians might 'sin twice against philosophy'. His will, preserved by Diogenes, makes thoughtful provision for his household slaves as well as his relatives, and, in the words of a recent biographer, 'affords the clearest evidence of a grateful and affectionate nature'.

Writings

In his earlier Platonising period Aristotle published a series of philosophical dialogues mainly on ethical themes. These works gained him a reputation as a popular writer with an elegant style, but they have largely perished. His fame now rests on a series of treatises of a very different character which he did not himself publish, and which seem to have remained largely unknown until the first century BC when a definitive edition was produced by Andronicus of Rhodes. These writings are conspicuously lacking in the stylistic graces that adorn the dialogues of Plato. Always terse and sometimes obscure, they occasionally contain passages that appear very rough and unfinished. No attempt is made to avoid repetitions, and the second treatment of a topic sometimes diverges appreciably from the first. The most likely explanation is that the treatises represent Aristotle's own memoranda composed after a lecture course as a considered statement of what he had said. The occasional inconsistencies would then be explained as 'second thoughts' when he came to give the same course again.

The following catalogue mentions nearly all the genuine extant works in the order in which they appear in the manuscript tradition:

(1) Works on logic
Aristotle's logical works came to be known as the *Organon*, or 'instrument' of thought. They include the *Categories* (on types of predicate), *On Interpretation* (on judgement and propositions), and *Sophistic Refutations* (on fallacies). Aristotle's central and totally original contribution to logic (not a term that he used himself) was the doctrine of the syllogism. His 'syllogistic' aimed to provide a general account of the process of deductive inference. It was worked out in definitive detail in the *Prior Analytics*. This work founded the science of formal logic and also expounded it in a form that held the field until our own century. Not the least significant of its innovations was the use of the letters A, B, C, and so on, to stand for general terms, enabling him to set out formal patterns of inference.

(2) Works on natural science (Physics)
These include the *Physics* proper in eight books, together with treatises on the heavens, on 'generation and corruption', and on meteorology. Physics for Aristotle was the science of 'natural bodies' which can exist separately but are not unchangeable. By his systematic study of how such bodies are produced, how they move and change, and how they are destroyed, Aristotle formulated a world system which totally dominated scientific thought until the Renaissance.

(3) Works on psychology
The series is headed by a general work in three books *On the Soul*, and includes special studies of sensation, memory, sleep, and so on.

(4) Works on biology
Because of his detailed researches into the animal kingdom Aristotle ranks as the leading naturalist of the ancient world. The extensive *Enquiry into Animals* constitutes a general introduction to zoology. Aristotle identified 495 species, outlining a scheme of classification, and noting different ways of reproduction, for example, by live birth, by egg, by larvae. The work contains a large collection of facts about animals, including much detailed observation of insects and fishes. Three other monographs deal with the parts, movement, and generation of animals.

(5) Works on metaphysics
A number of philosophical essays begun and revised by Aristotle at various stages of his career were finally collected and published in antiquity (though not by Aristotle) under the general and non-committal title of '*Meta-Phusika**'. The term simply means 'Works after the *Physics*', a reference to their position in the standard ancient edition of his works. It is the content of the essays that has determined our use of the term 'metaphysics', a term which Aristotle himself did not use. His own preferred name was 'first philosophy'.

The heart of the treatise lies in Books 6, 7, and 8 which develop Aristotle's concept of Being as Substance, and discuss the philosophical interpretation of matter and change. From its wide range and long-lasting influence, particularly on mediaeval thought, the *Metaphysics* must have a good claim to be the most important philosophical treatise ever written.

(6) Works on ethics
The *Eudemian* and *Nicomachean Ethics* (*ethika**) are probably the editions of Aristotle's ethical thought made by his friend Eudemus and his son Nicomachus respectively. There are still unsolved problems about the precise relationship between them, but the *Eudemian* is probably the earlier. The ten books of the *Nicomachean Ethics* represent one of the finest contributions ever made to the subject.

113

(7) Works on politics
Like the *Metaphysics*, the *Politics* is a collection of originally independent essays. It contains penetrating and memorable reflections
on the nature and organisation of the Greek *polis*, and remains a
seminal work in the evolution of political theory.

(8) Works of literary criticism
These consist of three books on *Rhetoric*, and one book on *Poetics*,
dealing with tragedy and epic. A sequel on comedy has been lost.

In their scope and originality the treatises represent an intellectual achievement that has never been equalled, let alone surpassed.
Not for nothing did Dante call Aristotle 'the master of those who
know'. If, as seems likely from internal evidence, most of them were
composed in his second Athenian period when head of the Lyceum
(*c.*335–323), they also testify to an almost superhuman energy and
facility of expression. In these twelve years Aristotle established the
broad lines along which intellectual enquiry has proceeded ever
since. He had something significant to say on most of the major
subjects currently taught in modern universities. While his pupil
Alexander was away conquering the world, Aristotle in Athens was
mapping out the territory of an intellectual empire that was to have
even more durable and influential effects in the cultural history of
mankind.

Thought: perception and knowledge
'If we did not perceive anything we would not learn or understand anything.'

By sayings like this Aristotle is indicating his firm belief that
sense-perception is the basis of knowledge. Here he stood in complete opposition to Plato, who distrusted the senses as a source of
illusion and denied that perception constitutes knowledge in any
way at all. For Aristotle, a creature endowed with the capacity of
sensing is able to perceive particular facts about real objects and is
thus able to discriminate features of the external world. But mind
must come into play if knowledge is to result. He would have agreed
with Kant's remark that 'sense without thought is blind'. What we
perceive must be retained in the memory for comparison with
future perceptions. On the basis of a mass of similar memories we
become experienced in certain perceptual situations and are able to

make generalisations and predictions about our environment. A 'red sky in the morning' becomes a 'shepherd's warning'. That somewhat rudimentary form of knowledge called weather lore is the outcome of a large number of observations from which a general rule is inferred. The rule is not yet a part of scientific knowledge because it does not supply an explanation of the phenomenon, but it is on the way to becoming knowledge.

Besides induction there was also, for Aristotle, an intuitive factor in the scientific ordering of perceptual experience. He recognised that a universal explanation may suddenly dawn on the scientific mind as a result of one significant perceptual experience. Good examples of this can be found in Archimedes's discovery of specific gravity as he watched his bath overflow, or Darwin's recognition of the principle of natural selection in the finches of the Galapagos. The intuitive leap is possible because there is a universal element in every perceptual situation.

Aristotle thought that the sciences could and should be built up on the basis of observation refined by generalisation. He himself founded zoology by observing and classifying individual specimens. He was an assiduous collector of all kinds of data. He also lost no opportunity to broaden the basis of his experience by consulting experts in special fields and by reading as widely as possible. He took widespread and 'reputable' opinions seriously, realising that such consensus may be based on genuine insight. In all this he adopted a genuinely empirical approach to knowledge.

Philosophy as the knowledge of first causes: the four types of cause

'All human beings have a natural desire for knowledge' is the firm empirical generalisation that stands at the start of the *Metaphysics*, and there has never been a more devoted seeker after knowledge than Aristotle. He explains how philosophy arose from curiosity about the world, and states that the knowledge which will satisfy this sense of wonder is desired for its own sake and not for any ulterior motive. Myth-making also arose from primitive wonderment, and so 'the lover of myth is a kind of philosopher'. But the first philosophers went beyond the mythological stage of thought in their quest for a fully rational explanation of the origin of things.

Such an explanation must be a causal explanation, so philosophy for Aristotle amounts to a search for knowledge of the ultimate causes of things. He elaborated a fundamental doctrine that there are basically four types of cause, and four types only: material cause, efficient cause, formal cause, and final cause. These causes are the principles which determine the origin, existence, and intelligibility of any given object.

To state the material cause of an object is to state the bodily constituents out of which a thing comes into existence and which are present in it as a product. Its efficient cause is the immediate means by which it was brought into existence. Its formal cause is stated when one states the pattern or formula of what it is to be the object in question, for example, that the form of the octave is the ratio 2:1 in sound waves. Its final cause is the end, purpose, or goal, for which it was made or came into existence.

The meaning of these various types of cause may be illustrated with reference to a man-made object like a votive statue. One can be said to have fully explained the statue when one has stated : (1) that it is made of bronze (material cause); (2) that it was designed and cast by a sculptor (efficient cause); (3) that it represents an athlete (formal cause); (4) that it was made and set up to commemorate and glorify an Olympic victor (final cause).

The four types together constitute a complete analysis of all the conditions necessary for the coming into existence of an object or event, and so provide scientific knowledge of it. One must stress that in Aristotelian usage a statement of a thing's cause is a statement of what it essentially is, as well as a statement of how it has come to be. It is an analysis of static elements as well as moving factors, and constitutes a complete answer to the question why a thing is what it is.

The doctrine has universal application in science and philosophy, and Aristotle illustrates its cosmic dimensions from the theories of his predecessors. He holds that the Milesians were too limited in their approach because they sought for the explanation of the natural world in terms of its material constituents only. The Pythagoreans went to the other extreme by emphasising number and proportion (the formal cause) at the expense of matter. Anaxagoras introduced an important new principle of explanation when he set up cosmic Mind as the efficient cause of the origin of motion, and so of the world as we know it. Plato, he says, used only formal and material causes in his cosmology. Aristotle believed that his own philosophy represented the culmination of previous Greek speculation about the world because he alone paid due attention to all four types of cause.

The conceptual basis of knowledge

(A) Particular and universal

Plato regarded particulars as less real than universals (Forms). Aristotle adopted a radically different approach to the particular/ universal relationship. For Aristotle particulars such as God, Socrates, and my dog Toby are the only entities that have a separate and substantial existence. They are individuals, and the individual is a distinct substance in which qualities and attributes inhere. As such, the individual is the ultimate subject of meaningful sentences, and therefore the focus of 'truth'. Every descriptive statement must contain at least one universal, and a very common type of statement is that in which a universal is predicated of a particular. I say, for example, 'Toby is a dog', meaning that he shares a complex of qualities with other dogs. Toby is a particular; 'dogness' or 'canine nature' is a universal. His canine nature is more than just the way I view him. Aristotle regarded his canine nature as something objective and real, but a reality that did not exist apart from the various particular dogs which embody it. It is not a 'one apart from the many' (a Platonic Form), but a 'one throughout the many' (an Aristotelian essence).

(B) Potentiality and actuality

These terms figure largely in Aristotle's account of change. A 'potentiality' is the capacity of an object to pass from one state to another. A man asleep is potentially a man awake; a man with his eyes shut is potentially a seeing man; a mass of bronze is potentially a statue — in ways which a corpse, a blind man, and a bucket of water are not. In general, A can change to B because some of the conditions of B-ness are already inherent in it. A ripe apple soon becomes a rotten apple.

Potentiality is a necessary concept for explaining how change occurs, but change cannot be explained by it alone. The concept of actuality must also be invoked. The actual is the realisation of the potential, exhibiting a perfection which supervenes on imperfection. In the order of thought actuality is prior to potentiality because the potential can only be raised to the level of the actual by the agency of something actual. The potential is rooted in the actual and presupposes it. For example, if I now have the potential of learning more than I now know, it is because I already do know something. The actual is also shown to be prior to the potential by the consideration that it is eternal and imperishable (as form), while the potential (as matter) is more or less infected with mutability. A material object can change its place, it can alter in size or quality, and it can cease to exist. But the actuality which it possesses or exhibits, being an essential or formal characteristic, is by its very nature immune from alteration or destruction.

Aristotle is here in effect distinguishing two ways in which any given object may be regarded. If you are looking at an object from the standpoint of its history, you will look first, in the order of time, at the capacity or imperfect condition in it which preceded the realised activity or prime condition. The embryo is historically prior to the adult. But if you are considering the real or essential nature of an object apart from its process of development, you will look first, in the order of thought, at the actuality it embodies. The adult is philosophically prior to the embryo. This is the teleological approach so characteristic of Aristotle. For him the acorn is explained by the oak, and the chicken definitely comes before the egg.

(C) Matter and form
The linked but opposed concepts of matter and form figure very prominently in Aristotle's analysis of the world. At the top of the pyramid of reality are certain pure forms such as God, and also the 'intelligences' that move and direct the celestial spheres from without. But at every lower level all bodies include some matter, and their substance consists of a blend of matter and form. The matter and form of physical objects can be distinguished in thought, but are not found separately in reality. Unlike pure form, matter cannot exist on its own. It provides the substratum on which form is imposed, and it does this at various levels, so it is always relative to form, and must be re-defined in relation to form at each level. Bodies vary in complexity, and as one moves up the scale, the formal aspect of the lower and simpler body becomes the material aspect of the higher and more complex. For example, to the metallurgist bronze is the form which he produces by alloying the matter of copper and tin in the right proportions, but to the sculptor bronze is the matter on which he imposes the form of his statue.

The 'simple bodies', or 'elements', Fire, Air, Earth, and Water, are at the bottom of the scale, but even they are to some extent complex in that they consist of a substratum of 'prime matter' which has been given a certain form by the presence of certain pairs of the primary 'opposites', heat, cold, dryness, and fluidity. At a somewhat higher level of organisation come minerals like gold, and living tissues such as flesh and sinews. The tissues in turn provide the material for more highly formed parts such as the eye or the liver. The animal is a still more complex unity in which the formal element is represented by 'life' or 'soul' and the material element by organs and tissues.

Form, like matter, is found at various levels of complexity, and has a corresponding range of meanings. It sometimes means no more than 'visible shape', as in the case of a statue. But more often Aristotle uses 'form' in the sense of the 'inner nature' or 'intelligible structure' of a thing. The form can be stated in a formula or definition (*logos*). It constitutes the permanent 'essence' of a thing which persists though other aspects of it may change. Socrates, for example, has a permanent essence as a 'rational animal', though the colour of his hair or the strength of his limbs may vary at different stages of his life.

Aristotle on substance

In reply to the question 'Where is Socrates?' one might say that he is in the gymnasium, or the market-place, or his house. These are all places where he might be found, so all the answers fall into the same category, that of *place*. If asked what sort of man is he, one might say stubborn, or intelligent, or humorous, answering in the category of *quality*. These questions presuppose that there is an entity called Socrates who exhibits various qualities and can be found in different places at different times. They are not the ultimate question about Socrates. This must be the question 'What is Socrates?' and to that the ultimate answer is: 'A man (human being)'. Aristotle classifies this answer under the category of substance, and puts that category at the head of his list of categories.

Aristotle gives some rather unconvincing reasons for the priority of substance. In the last analysis it seems that he just felt that individual things are substances, and that their substantiality is the primary and absolute fact of their being, taking priority over any qualities they may possess or any relations they may enter into. In a famous phrase he remarks that 'the eternal question "What is being?" really amounts to the question "What is substance?"'.

His main problem, then, is to try to define the substantial element in an individual thing, and on this point he develops powerful arguments for equating substance with essence, or formal cause. It has been agreed that it is substance which makes things what they are. And if we ask, for example, what is it that makes this collection of materials into a house, the answer must be that they serve as a shelter for human beings and their goods, that is, they have the form of a house. This is their formal cause or essence. A house is a man-made object which embodies the purpose of its maker. So in this instance (as with all artefacts) the formal cause is the same as the final cause. The house shelters the people in it because it was designed to do so.

The essence of a thing must not be understood in any materialistic way. It is not another material component in addition to those already existing as part of the thing. Nor does it consist of material components. As immanent form it has an immaterial nature. It is the principle of structure, the principle which turns a mere collection of materials into an organised whole. As Aristotle says, the syllable BA is more than just the element A added to the element B. It is a new compound with a structure of its own, and it ceases to exist when broken down into its elements just as surely as a house ceases to exist when reduced to a heap of rubble. The elements are the material constituents into which substances are resolved when they lose their substantiality.

The structure of the universe
Aristotle did not have the problem of explaining the origin of the physical universe because he regarded it as eternal, but he had something significant to say about every other aspect of it. In his physical treatises he gave an account of its structure and components that was the accepted view of all thinking people until the rise of modern astronomy based on the work of Copernicus and Galileo.

There was, in his view, only one universe, spherical in shape and finite in extent. He rejected the atomic theory of matter and the notion of void. Bodies, he thought, could be divided anywhere, but could not ultimately be dissociated into atoms, and he viewed matter as extending in a continuum throughout the universe, leaving no absolutely empty space.

At the centre of the universe he located the globe of the earth, fixed and unmoving. He accepted contemporary estimates of its circumference at some 40,000 miles (64,000 kilometres), which he thought small in relation to the size of the other heavenly bodies. He argued strongly for its spherical shape, partly on the grounds that heavy bodies tend towards the centre and will naturally form themselves into a sphere, and partly from perceived indications such as the curved shadow cast in eclipses, and the substantial alterations in the star-map as one moves quite short distances to north or south. He correctly inferred that these alterations are due to the marked surface curvature of the quite small sphere from which we make our observations of the heavens.

The terrestrial globe, he thought, is largely composed of the element earth (which is cold and dry), and has on its surface water (which is cold and fluid). It is enveloped by the third element air (which is hot and fluid), and surrounding that again is the sphere of fire (which is hot and dry). The element earth has a natural tendency to sink, and so has moved down to occupy the centre of the universe, coming to rest there in a fixed and motionless mass. The element fire, on the other hand, has a natural tendency to rise, and so has moved outwards to its present position. But the natural movement of the elements has not resulted in their total separation, and they continue to interpenetrate each other to a considerable extent. When they make contact, one element is capable of transforming another, and this is a major cause of natural change. Empedocles, he thought, was wrong to regard the four Roots as immutable. For instance, when fire meets air, the fluidity of air may modify the dryness of fire to such an extent that all or some of the fire actually becomes air. Again, water and earth have an affinity through their coldness, and when they come in contact either may be transformed into the other by a tilt in the balance between their respective fluidity and dryness.

Natural species on the surface of the globe, such as plants and animals, are composed of varying amounts of the four elements. As composite sensible substances they are liable to four kinds of change: (1) they come into being and pass out of being (change of substance); (2) they change colour, ripen, grow soft or hard, etc. (change of quality); (3) they grow larger or smaller (change of quantity); (4) they move around (change of place). The ultimate efficient cause of these changes is the sun, or more specifically the movements of the sun as it alternately approaches and recedes from the earth in its annual progress through the sky.

All these types of change except the last are confined to the terrestrial or sublunary sphere. Above the sphere of the moon a different order of being is found in which there are substances that are sensible but eternal. These are the heavenly bodies, sun, moon, planets, and stars. They do not include any of the four terrestrial elements in their composition, but are made of a fifth and superior element (*quint*-essence) called ether. Ether is unlike the other elements in that it contains no 'opposites', and it does not admit of any change or alteration except change of place. It moves, but only in circles.

Stars and planets are imperishable and so 'divine', and he agreed with Plato that their motion must always conform to the pattern of perfect motion, namely, motion in a circle. Since the planets did not appear to conform to this requirement Plato proposed to his colleagues in the Academy the problem of devising a theory to 'save the appearances'. This was to be done by demonstrating that apparent deviations such as the retrograde movement of the planets in relation to the constellations were illusory and not real. The desired result was achieved by positing a complicated system of concentric spheres carrying the heavenly bodies, with their poles inclined at different angles, and rotating with different velocities. By an amazing feat of mathematical calculation the observed motions were then explained in terms of resolutions of the real circular motions.

Aristotle accepted the principle of this explanation, and posited no fewer than fifty-five spheres to sustain it. The outermost sphere was the heaven of the fixed stars, rotating unceasingly with a very high velocity, and communicating this motion downwards and inwards through the lower spheres.

At this point Aristotle's physics and astronomy merged with his theology. He argued that the primary motion of the outermost heaven could not be produced without the existence of an eternal substance whose very being is actuality, and which is therefore totally immaterial. This line of reasoning led him to his famous conception of the Unmoved Mover, God, who is pure Form unmixed with any matter. God is not a part of the universe, and is not in space or motion. But God is the ultimate cause of motion, for the heaven of fixed stars yearns towards God, and this longing for God, this desire to come as near as possible to the beauty and perfection of pure Form, sets up the circular motion of the outer-most sphere. Aristotle summed up his theory in a celebrated phrase which proved a major source of inspiration to Dante:

> He causes motion as an object of desire, and the heaven which
> is moved moves everything else.

This purely rational proof of the existence of God is a variant of the argument from the contingency of the world to a necessary first cause. It emphasises the 'pull from in front', the pull of form on matter, of the actual on the potential, and represents the culmination of his teleological mode of thought.

Since God is immaterial, God's activity must be intellectual, and He must contemplate the best possible object, which cannot be other than Himself. Thought when fully actualised possesses and coalesces with its object, so God as the 'thinking of thinking' coalesces with Himself. He is Thought thinking itself. But in Aristotle's conception he is more than Thought, for the actuality of thought is life, and God as actuality must be actively alive.

> We say then that God is a living being, eternal, perfect in
> goodness; life and duration, continuous and eternal, pertain
> to God; for that is what God is.

The God of Aristotle is not a creator God since the world co-exists eternally with Him. It is not said that He takes any interest in the world or bears love towards mankind. Like the gods of Epicurus, He exists above and beyond the world in a transcendent state of blissful self-contemplation, coldly detached to our way of thinking. But for Aristotle the goodness of things in our sublunary world is ultimately derived from Him, since He is the end or goal towards which they strive as they seek to develop away from the mere potentiality of matter towards the realisation of form.

Practical philosophy

(A) The nature of well-being (happiness)
In his treatises on practical philosophy Aristotle made it his aim to set out the conditions of human well-being, and to state how this 'good' might be realised in the individual and in society. His *Ethics* is a study of the factors in character which conduce to the happiness or well-being (*eudaimonia**) of the individual. The *Politics* exam-

ines how political communities should be organised in order to achieve the 'good for man'. This good is the same in kind for the individual and the citizen body. It is better than nothing if it can be secured for the individual, but the science of politics does not fully realise itself unless the good is shared by the whole community.

I shall concentrate on the *Ethics* because I think it contains a great deal of material that is still very relevant for the study of conduct. The *Politics* is of great historical interest, but is inevitably somewhat dated in so far as its perspective is largely bounded by the conditions of the Greek *polis*. However, it still remains valuable for its analysis of the nature of citizenship, and for its account of various types of constitution from monarchy to democracy. Aristotle's remarks on the 'middle class' as a stabilising influence in the community are of particular interest, and he had an acute perception of the nature of the class struggle in his day between rich (oligarchs) and poor (democrats). In theory he favours the 'rule of the best', but in practice he seems to incline to democratic forms as more likely to ensure the 'rule of law', a point of view well summed up in his pithy remark: 'The diners are a better judge of the meal than the cook.'

Aristotle took it as axiomatic that every action aims at achieving some good, and that there must be a *summum bonum*, or supreme good, which is the ultimate goal of human activity. He accepts the common perception that this supreme good is 'happiness' or 'well-being'. I prefer 'well-being' as a rendering of the Greek *eudaimonia* because in our modern world 'happiness' tends to be equated with momentary elation, or joy, or the temporary euphoria associated with 'being in love'. In so far as such states are pleasant Aristotle would not decry them, but he is looking for a more solid and permanent basis for human contentment.

Pleasure, he thinks, is an element in well-being, but does not constitute its essence, and pleasure-seeking should not be made the main aim of life. He also dismisses the notion that a life devoted to money-making will of itself produce well-being. Reasonable prosperity is a precondition of felicity, but wealth cannot be the supreme good because it is essentially a means to other goods. Nor can 'honour' (in the sense of recognition by society) be the supreme good, because it is an external good bestowed by others, while well-being must spring from within one's personality.

He reaches his own conception of well-being by viewing human life in the perspective of all life. Plants and animals are also alive and share the functions of nutrition and reproduction with humans. Animals and humans stand on a higher level than plants because they can perceive and move, but the power of perception and movement is in no way confined to humans. Aristotle then asks whether there is any power or function which is typical of human beings alone, and which serves to distinguish mankind from the animal kingdom. He finds this distinctive feature in man's ability to reason which is shown both in his response to reason and his exercise of reason. Since the active rational element is peculiar to man, it serves to define his proper function, which is to live actively in accordance with reason.

A good man is one who successfully fulfils his function, and so fulfils himself. He does this by living up to the highest excellence of which he is capable, which means that he lives well, and so achieves well-being.

The main points of the discussion are then gathered together in a formal definition of the good for man, which reads as follows:

> The good for man [well-being or happiness] is an activity of the soul in accordance with its own excellence [that is, in accordance with virtue].

The definition is completed by the addition of the phrase 'in a complete life' to reinforce the point that a moment of happiness does not constitute well-being.

Aristotle has now met the challenge of defining the essence of well-being, but accepts that his definition provides an outline-sketch only, and that it needs to be given body by a discussion of the nature of the human excellences or virtues in accordance with which human activity must proceed.

But before proceeding to this discussion he tests his definition by comparing it with accepted beliefs about human felicity. This is typical of his method. He regards himself as refining rather than rejecting common-sense views. The definition holds up because it finds well-being in the soul rather than in external or bodily goods. It also allows for pleasure as a component in well-being because pleasure is related to activity. But its chief merit is to stress that activity is the very essence of well-being. This is in line with Olympic practice where the crown is given, not to the most hand-some competitor, but to the one who competes and wins.

(B) Moral excellence: the golden mean

Aristotle regarded the moral virtues as dispositions or aptitudes for action which were acquired by training and perfected by practice. He compared them to the skills of a craftsman or an artist. Just as a man becomes a builder by building houses or a musician by playing musical instruments, so he becomes brave by doing brave actions and temperate by doing temperate ones. He stressed the importance of habituation in developing moral excellence. People are not born good, but they are born with the capacity to become good, and will do so if they build up the appropriate dispositions by repeated performance of the right actions.

To be moral, such actions must be done consciously and deliberately, and must be chosen for their own sake, but the most important condition of all is that the actions should issue from a habit-fixed disposition of the mind or character. One generous action does not entitle a person to be called generous. It might have been done on impulse; it might even have been a mistake. The actions of a generous person are predictable because they stem from a generous habit of mind. In the same way the actions of a good games player are predictable because he has acquired the skill to react appropriately in a given situation. The same analysis applies to all the moral virtues from generosity up to justice.

How does one know when the virtuous disposition has been established? A crucial test is the amount of pleasure or pain that attends the action. If you do not like being generous, or find it hard to be temperate, you have not acquired the virtue though you may do the virtuous action. If on the other hand you enjoy the practice of the virtue in question, then you have acquired that particular excellence. Pleasure is the test of a formed habit. Punctual people like being punctual!

The next problem is to find a criterion for assessing what is the right or virtuous action in any given situation, and Aristotle solves this by his celebrated doctrine of the 'golden mean', as it came to be called. A 'mean' is literally a 'mid-point'; it implies extremes. An objective mean can be arithmetically determined, but in the actions which make up conduct account must be taken of subjective factors. For example, what is too much food for me may be too little for a vigorous athlete. Nevertheless even a subjective mean lies between its own extremes. Aristotle adduces various reasons why one should aim at the mean in conduct. There is the common-sense

126

consideration that extremes tend to be harmful or even destructive. Too much food or exercise can be as bad for a person as too little. The mean adjusted to the person's needs produces health. There is the aesthetic consideration. The master of any art or skill avoids excess or defect, and chooses what is intermediate. It is the mark of a good work of art that nothing can be added to it or removed from it without spoiling it. It is just right. Finally there is the criterion of success or failure. There are many ways of getting a sum wrong, only one way of getting it right. Success in finding the mean is difficult, failure all too easy. The moral agent in any given situation may be compared to an archer aiming at a target. It is easy to over-shoot or fall short; the hard thing is to hit the mark, but that constitutes success.

In the light of all these considerations it becomes clear that the mean is the appropriate *form* which the moral agent imposes on the matter of moral action. As such, it constitutes the essence or formal cause of a moral action. The efficient cause of the action is the deliberate choice of the agent to act or react in a certain way. His choice must be freely made and he must understand what he is doing. The material cause is the raw material of action which consists either of spontaneous and unformed emotions such as anger, fear, pity, or basic actions such as eating, talking, getting, spending, praising, blaming. These are the ingredients which may be present in conduct to excess, or in deficiency. The timid man feels more fear than is appropriate to the danger, the rash man not enough. The irascible man reacts too vigorously when provoked. Criticism can be phrased too strongly or not strongly enough. In all these cases the excess of the emotion or the action constitutes a fault or vice, and so at the other extreme does the defect. The hard thing is to hit the mean: to find or feel the delicate sense of danger, proper pride, righteous anger, the right word at the right moment.

The mean is determined by right reason as embodied in the man of practical wisdom. It does not represent a compromise between two vices, but an essentially correct solution to a practical problem. Once it is determined the vices of excess and defect take shape in relation to it. For example, the courageous man deliberates and chooses a certain appropriate course of action in response to impending danger, and his action embodies the virtue of courage. Those who deviate markedly from his response are deemed to be either rash or cowardly.

(C) Intellectual excellence

Intellectual excellence is an even more important component of the good life than moral excellence. Aristotle holds that we need prudence, or practical wisdom, to assess correctly the factors in any situation where moral action is required. It is the virtue which enables us to select the right means to achieve our desired goals. As such, it deals with concrete situations and problems which call for deliberation, and operates in the sphere of contingent fact. Like the moral virtues, it is a disposition to make good choices, and it can be improved and strengthened by practice. It is a virtue of the fully rational part of the soul.

Socrates looked on all the virtues as processes of reasoning or forms of knowledge. Aristotle criticised this approach as over-intellectual. In his opinion Socrates did not pay enough attention to irrational or semi-rational factors in morality such as appetite and habit. But to some extent he went along with Socrates in treating a person's moral character as a totality of dispositions whose unity is formed by practical wisdom.

But there is another excellence of the rational soul which Aristotle values even more highly than practical wisdom. This is speculative, or theoretical, wisdom which operates in the sphere of what is universal and necessary rather than contingent. With its aid we contemplate the noblest aspects of the world and grasp truths about its eternal nature and constitution. This type of wisdom goes beyond practical wisdom, whose object is limited to achieving the good for man. It is the specific excellence of the philosopher who raises his eyes to the heavenly sphere and attempts to understand the world as a whole.

Aristotle accepted that philosophers may be less practical than men whose vision is more limited. The philosopher may know that light meats are easily digestible and so wholesome, but may not be good at recognising such meats in the market. The man who simply knows that chicken is wholesome may achieve a healthier diet. He also mentions another interesting indication of the difference between the two types of wisdom. Young prodigies in mathematics (and we could add, chess) appear from time to time, but one never sees teenage statesmen. This is because mathematical ability (and skill at chess) depends on insight into form and structure and the ability to calculate quickly and logically. Statesmanship requires a more mature experience of life and human nature than is possible for a young person. Again we see Aristotle diverging from Plato on this point. Plato's philosopher-king has to become a highly trained metaphysician before he is allowed to administer a state. Aristotle accepts that skill in practical politics depends on a different type of intellectual ability from that of the scientist or philosopher.

Though Aristotle was an acute student of politics, his heart was in the life of contemplation rather than action. He waxes unusually eloquent in describing the happiness which a life devoted to philosophic contemplation can bring. The highest part of human nature is reason, and the noblest part of reason is the theoretical or speculative part. To be active, and successful, in theorising is to realise the highest excellence of which human beings are capable, and therefore constitutes the highest form of well-being. Of all human activities it is the least likely to be impeded and the most likely to be self-perpetuating. A life devoted to contemplative reasoning fulfils the two necessary conditions of felicity: it is self-sufficient, and it is self-desirable. By contrast a life devoted to political or military activity is unleisurely and aims at ulterior ends. Intellectual activity can be pursued in leisure and without fatigue. If a perfect length of life is accorded to it, it will be beyond doubt the absolutely happy life for man.

In a sense, Aristotle thinks, such a life will be too good for human beings. They will enjoy it in virtue of a more than human element in their make-up, the element of divine reason. They should not pay attention to the traditional Greek advice to play safe, to think mortal thoughts, and not to meddle with high matters.

> So far as in him lies a human being should seek immortality, and should exert himself to live in accordance with the dominant element in his nature.

Somewhat paradoxically, Aristotle suggests that this element, which he has just called divine, is a person's true self, and that a life devoted to intellectual enquiry is the proper life for a human being, 'if it is true that the intellect more than anything else is the man'. This argument is the culmination of Aristotle's scientific humanism.

Epilogue

Plato's *Republic* exhibits a varied and charming blend of psychology, ethics, political theory, and metaphysics, all designed to attract and inspire the reader. Aristotle's approach was very different. He believed in sticking to one subject at a time, aiming at a methodical and complete analysis of each topic, and a down-to-earth clarity of exposition. Unlike Plato, he did not regard 'first philosophy' as the apex of the sciences, with certainty as its prime requirement. In his *Metaphysics* he generally favours a very undogmatic approach, raising problems as much as suggesting solutions, and using careful analysis of meaning to extract a more precise formulation of truth from received but loosely worded views.

One of his most enduring contributions was his development of philosophical terminology. When we use distinctions and antitheses like universal and particular, premise and conclusion, subject and attribute, form and matter, potential and actual, we are employing tools of thought that were first forged by Aristotle.

He was reluctant to advance or support any view that was flagrantly at variance with common sense, but at the same time his speculations were far from trite or obvious. He almost always managed to impose a powerfully novel interpretation on any body of material that he handled. The bias of his mind was empirical rather than idealistic. He was a true successor to the early Ionians in his devotion to research and his concentration on particular objects in the external world. 'In every product of nature', he said, 'there is something to arouse our wonder.'

10

THE HELLENISTIC SCHOOLS: STOICS, EPICUREANS, AND SCEPTICS

THE POLITICAL CHARACTER of the Hellenistic Age has been out-lined in the Introduction (p.11). The sudden expansion of the Greek world brought about by Alexander's victories inevitably created something of a religious and cultural vacuum. The older gods and traditions began to seem less and less relevant to the new rivalries of big power politics. People wanted new codes and creeds to live by, and the need was largely supplied by the two great new philosophical systems of Stoicism and Epicureanism.

Both systems originated in Athens at the start of the third century BC, both spread quickly and widely, and both became influential in Roman circles as Roman power spread eastwards from the mid-second century BC onwards. Each was a well-organised and richly textured compilation of ideas which drew heavily on the treasures of previous Greek speculation. Each was primarily an ethical system, sharply focused on the individual, and providing its adherents with a set of precepts by which they could order and direct their lives. Though each was grounded in a distinctively different view of the nature of the external world, the practical outcome of each for conduct was not too dissimilar. Each was a consistently rational attempt to solve the problems of man's relationship with his environment, and each claimed to provide a formula for happy and contented living.

Both systems possessed a universal appeal because they broke with the more old-fashioned and limiting circumstances of city-state life. Stoicism was in tune with the 'cosmopolitanism' of the new age, Epicureanism with its 'individualism'. The Epicurean was required to pledge allegiance to Epicurus as his sole master and mentor. This new loyalty to a person freed him from older civic ties which were no longer helpful or appropriate. It left him free to pursue his personal happiness in a cloistered seclusion from an alien political world that he could no longer control or comprehend. The Stoic could also transcend old loyalties with his cosmopolitan claim to membership of the human race, a concept fostered by the new welding of mankind promoted by Alexander's conquests. He was no longer just an Athenian or a Spartan, but a 'citizen of the world', not subject to local laws and customs, but obedient to the universal rule of reason and natural law.

The third main Hellenistic school, Scepticism, developed, in part at least, in reaction to the dogmatic views of the other schools, and it too promised peace of mind to its adherents in return for opting out of the quest for what was regarded as unattainable knowledge.

THE STOICS

The Stoic School

The Stoic School was founded in Athens at the end of the fourth century by a Cypriot named Zeno. Zeno (335–263) arrived in Athens in 313 and there came strongly under the influence of the Cynics, who were followers of Socrates. He then developed his own system, which he began to expound publicly from about 300 onwards. He used to lecture in a centrally placed portico (*stoa**) called the Painted Porch, and the name 'Stoic' is derived from this fact. Zeno was much admired and respected by the Athenians, and the disciples whom he attracted formed themselves into the Stoic School. The School was never as tightly organised as the Academy, but it continued in existence under a succession of heads down at least until AD260.

From the start Stoicism was a dogmatic system, and Zeno established it under the three main headings of logic, physics, and ethics. In Stoic circles philosophy was compared to a fruitful field surrounded by the fence of logic. The fence was designed to ward off the attacks of the sceptic by showing that knowledge of reality is possible. The soil of the field stood for physics, a subject which the philosopher was expected to cultivate in order to gain an understanding of the nature of the world. The crop was the type of conduct expected from the Stoic wise man in whom reason ruled and emotion was suppressed. We still use 'stoical' to characterise someone who remains unperturbed by triumph or disaster.

Stoic doctrine

(A) Logic

The term 'logic' appears to have been a Stoic coinage, and the early Stoics were subtle logicians whose work on the nature of propositions and inference has attracted interest and respect from modern experts in symbolic logic.

There was, however, a broader and less technical side to their logic, a side which would now be called theory of knowledge. Following the example of Aristotle, the Stoics set out to provide an empirical justification of knowledge by grounding it in valid perceptions, and then tracing the psychological stages by which such perceptions are transformed into assured knowledge.

They began by positing the existence of external objects which operate on the senses to produce 'appearances' in the mind. (They also recognised that the mind can generate 'ideas', or mental appearances, by its own operation and independently of any direct stimulus from the senses.) The mind, they said, responds with 'assent' to the impressions produced through the senses when they clearly signify the presence of an object which can be comprehended. What makes an object comprehensible is the presence of 'clarity' or 'vividness' in the impressions it generates. This quality of 'clarity' is matched on the side of the perceiving subject by a response which they called 'comprehension'. Comprehension is a knowing response to a truly existent object, and is to be carefully distinguished from opinion which is not so securely grounded in the experience of the external. Comprehension provides the 'criterion of truth' (*kriterion**).

The empirical cast of Stoic epistemology cannot be over-emphasised. They anticipated Locke in describing the mind in infancy as a *tabula rasa*, or 'clean slate', on which impressions as they arise are recorded as in a ledger. Memory is built up out of these 'traces', and the mind becomes equipped with general notions through the activity of reason, which sorts the impressions and notes similarities between them.

In his public lectures Zeno used to illustrate the various stages from perception up to irrefutable knowledge by a series of gestures. He would first of all hold out one arm with the fingers of the hand open and parted. This symbolised the first tentative contact between the mind and the external world. Then he would begin to curl his fingers together to signify growing assent until finally fingers and thumb came together to 'make a fist'. This signified the moment of comprehension. Finally he would bring over his other hand and clasp the 'fist' in it to symbolise the function of philosophic reasoning in strengthening and securing knowledge to the point where it cannot be expunged from the mind. We owe the description of the scene to Cicero, and it brings us close in imagination to one of the great teachers of the ancient world.

(B) Physics

The Stoic view of the world was technically a materialistic one. They held that anything that really exists is corporeal. To act, or be acted upon, any existent thing must be furnished with a body. This applied to the human soul, and also to God. Even an 'abstract' moral quality like goodness was viewed as a state or condition of the material constituting the soul.

But they avoided a mechanistic view of the operations of nature. The world, they held, is the product of an active principle to which they gave various names, including Mind and God. They conceived of God as an active force, permeating the physical world, and fashioning its more passive material elements into an ordered world of separate objects. God consisted of the finest and most active forms of matter, namely fire and air, mixed together to produce a divine 'spirit' or 'fiery breath' which nourished the world from within. God goes about his work like a skilled craftsman. Hence the order and design that in their view were such significant aspects of reality. Hence also the cunning adaptation of the various parts of the organism to different purposes. They accepted the great Greek tradition of the world as a *cosmos*. But the analogy of the craftsman should not mislead us into separating the Stoic God from the material in which he works. For the Stoics, God was not above or outside the world imposing form on matter like a human designer. God was in the world and part of the world just as surely as soul was included in body. They proclaimed a pantheistic creed.

The Stoics viewed the cosmos as a living entity in which every part is organically connected to every other part. In the words of Cicero it 'feels and breathes together' like a vast organism. The parts of the universe are conjoined by a universal 'sympathy' which ensures that whatever happens in one place is felt through the whole. They pictured the body of the cosmos as guided by reason, which ensures that nothing happens at random. All is pre-ordained by fate. All is providentially controlled by the divine and rational spirit working in and through the world.

They followed Aristotle in conceiving the world as finite in extent and spherical in shape. Its material was not split up into atoms with empty space in between. The material of the Stoic world formed a continuum which was infinitely divisible, and which filled every part of the world, leaving no void. Their opponents argued that such a world would exclude the possibility of motion, but the Stoics said that the *plenum* is elastic, enfolding us as water enfolds fish, and so allowing living creatures the possibility of movement.

(C) Ethics

Their fundamental ethical maxim was that people should aim to live 'in accordance with nature', but this was no 'back to nature' movement. 'Nature' was understood as an ideally ordered world formed and guided by divine reason. So 'following nature' meant living up to one's true nature as a rational being. It also meant living in conformity with 'natural law'. Their doctrine was that man's situation in a rationally ordered world imposes certain duties on him, and he is required to respond by choosing to do what is morally and objectively good. Choice of the right action constitutes virtue, and will lead inevitably to happiness. Vice consists in choosing actions which are contrary to natural law.

Virtue, they held, is the only absolute good, and vice the only absolute evil. Between these extremes lie various objects of desire or aversion which are morally 'indifferent'. These include life and death, health and disease, pleasure and pain, beauty and ugliness, wealth and poverty. None of these is good or bad in itself; all are morally neutral since all can be used to promote or injure a person's true interests. The wisdom of the sage consists in his ability to distinguish between apparent and real good.

Since there is only one absolute good, virtue, and one absolute evil, vice, it follows that all good actions are equally good, and all vicious actions equally evil. It also follows that there is no scale of excellence in the grading of character. No person is morally good until he/she has reached moral perfection.

The Stoic exaltation of reason involved a corresponding depreciation of pleasure and emotion. They were basically anti-hedonist in their outlook, though some allowed that not all pleasures were contrary to nature. However, they generally took the view that the primary impulse of living creatures is to self-preservation, not to pleasure. Pleasure is never to be made an object of pursuit because it is not a natural end or motive of action but only a by-product of action. They classed pleasure with three other primary emotions, pain, fear, and hope. The emotions were all regarded with suspicion because they tend to disturb and upset the mind and make it lose the calmness and balance of reason. Their strictures were chiefly directed against the more violent emotions, but any emotion was regarded as a defect in the soul analogous to disease in the body.

These views were summed up in the ideal of *apatheia**, meaning 'absence of passion'. Stoic 'apathy' was far from exemplifying the modern sense of that word, which is now used to designate lack of interest and involvement. There was certainly an element of detachment in the Stoic attitude to life but it was not without vigour too. 'Apathy' was a state of mind in which one did one's duty without being in any way swayed by emotion. They thought that if one could achieve such a state one would be happy, because happiness consists in the absence of mental disturbance rather than the presence of bodily enjoyment.

This conception underlines the somewhat negative side which was undoubtedly a part of Stoic morality. 'Refrain and endure' was a typical maxim. They exhorted people to fortitude in order to get rid of anxiety, to self-control in order to free themselves from desire. They set great store by self-restraint and self-reliance because that made one independent of shifting fortune and all external influences.

The early Stoics were against emotion because they viewed it as incompatible with rational control. Zeno defined it as a movement of mind contrary to reason and nature, an 'impulse to excess'. Stoic psychological theory linked emotion with imagination, stating that most desires are based on false opinions of what is good or bad for us. Greed, for example, derives from a false assessment of the value of money. They concluded that just as one can and should get rid of false opinions, so one can and should get rid of emotions altogether.

Not surprisingly the more austere aspects of early Stoic ethics were later toned down. The complete rejection of emotion was modified to the extent that the wise man was allowed to experience certain 'permitted affections'. These included calm cheerfulness, reverence, and benevolence, which were held to be appropriate responses to the majesty of the universe and the needs of the human condition. Such affections or feelings were held to differ from emotion because they were deeply tinged with reason, and were not violent enough to disturb the general equanimity of the sage.

There was also a common-sense modification of the doctrine that virtue is the only good. In the realm of 'things indifferent' later Stoics distinguished between what was in accordance with nature, for example eyesight and health, and what was contrary to nature (because militating against self-preservation), for example, blindness and disease. Such a distinction at once confers a superior *value* on health, even if it does not make it into an absolute good. It would therefore be rational to choose what leads to health instead of what leads to disease, *provided no higher good suffers as a result*. Health was accounted one of the 'things preferred' because it has appreciable positive value short of being absolutely good. Disease, and what produces it, such as a bad diet and lack of exercise, has a negative value and so fell into the class of 'things to be avoided'. There was also a third class of 'things genuinely indifferent' such as whether to use one piece of money or another in settlement of a debt.

Social commitment and the ethics of suicide

Stoic ethics exhibited two main currents of thought which always tended to diverge. If emphasis was placed on the organic unity of the cosmos, it followed that the individual had a duty to adopt a cosmopolitan outlook and to exert himself for the common good of society. If the paramount worth of rational conduct was stressed, the values of inner freedom and individual self-sufficiency tended to take precedence over everything else.

There is much stress on the duty of social commitment in the thought of Marcus Aurelius, and this is not surprising given his responsibilities as head of the Roman Empire. His *Meditations* are full of pregnant sayings like 'Fellowship is the purpose behind our creation' and 'The mind of the universe is social'. He particularly emphasised the connection of each person with the community in a 'brotherhood of all rational beings'. In his view we have a duty to

137

subordinate our private interests to those of society. 'To obstruct one another is against Nature's law.' In one passage his language is quite reminiscent of St Paul when he speaks of each individual as a 'limb' or 'member' of the one body, and extols the joy of doing good to others.

The right of the individual to take his own life seems to stand at the opposite pole from the duty of social commitment. Consequently most religions condemn suicide as morally wrong, but the Stoics refused to do so. They regarded suicide as the ultimate assertion of individual freedom, and considered that man as a moral agent should be free to choose death instead of life. To do so for a good and compelling reason was in their view the ultimate triumph of the good will.

Law and the wise man
Stoic insistence on the importance of law made the creed particularly congenial to the Roman mind. Their conception of law sprang directly from their world view. They accepted that the divine reason immanent in the world has arranged all things in a providentially good way, and that everyone has a duty to conform to this arrangement. The arrangement in itself fosters certain attitudes and actions, such as respect for parents, care for children, and fair and humane treatment of fellow human beings. Now this, they pointed out, is precisely what human law does when it embodies and enjoins a code of conduct. For the Stoics, human law is a reflection of the 'divine' or 'natural' law inherent in the way things are. In their view everyone has a natural tendency to do what this law prescribes, and a natural aversion from doing what it forbids. Irrational impulses may tend to thwart these tendencies, but the wise man has suppressed all such impulses, and so he will obey the laws imposed on him by political authority (provided its laws are in accord with the natural law). He will also obey them freely because his own rational nature tells him to do so.

Stoicism was a strenuous system, and its devotees aimed at nothing less than perfection. The concept of the ideal wise man provided a standard which all were required to emulate, even if very few attained it. The Stoics liked to express the perfection of the wise man in paradoxical assertions. The wise man alone is beautiful because only virtue is beautiful. The wise man alone is rich because true riches consist in having no wants. The wise man is king because he is master of himself. His freedom from emotion and desire secures the wise man in a state of unruffled contentment. By contrast the fool is a prey to misery and discontent. By the strict Stoic standard almost the whole of mankind belonged to the class of the foolish. Only very rarely did a truly wise man, a Socrates, a Diogenes, a Cato, appear. They tended to see things in black and white terms. To lack any part of virtue was to lack it completely. One who is only an inch below the surface of the water, they said, will be drowned just the same as one who is 500 fathoms down.

The conception of the wise man enshrines the moral absolutism and idealism of the system. Stoicism was in many respects a heroic creed, and many of its adherents showed more than human disregard for danger and death. They found the strength to act as they did, not in the hope of future reward but from the settled conviction that virtue is its own reward since it alone is intrinsically good and desirable. Let Epictetus have the last word: 'The good man will not be a common thread in the fabric of humanity, but a purple thread — that touch of brilliance which gives distinction and beauty to the rest.'

THE EPICUREANS

The School of Epicurus
Epicurus (341–270) was an Athenian, born in the Athenian colony on Samos where his father Neocles was working as a schoolmaster. As a youth he was well-schooled in philosophy, and in 309 he began to teach the subject, first at Mytilene in Lesbos, and then at Lampsacus on the Hellespont.

In *c.*306/7 he returned to Athens, and bought there a house with a garden which became the headquarters of the Epicurean School. Apart from occasional visits to Asia Minor he remained in Athens as a teacher for the rest of his life. His School became known as 'The Garden' in symbolic distinction from 'The Porch'. The Stoics did not hesitate to immerse themselves in public affairs, but the Epicureans preferred a life of quiet seclusion.

Epicurus was a voluminous writer, whose works filled 300 papyrus rolls, but little has survived. Diogenes Laertius has preserved three Letters in which he summarised his philosophy for the benefit of friends, and a set of forty-three moral maxims known as the 'principal doctrines'. Some charred rolls of his treatise *On Nature* were recovered from a villa in Herculaneum, and eighty-one more maxims were discovered in a Vatican manuscript in 1888. Apart from these scattered scraps, we have the great poetic exposition of the Epicurean system by Lucretius.

Unlike Stoicism, Epicureanism did not undergo any later modifications. It persisted in its original form as established by Epicurus himself, and no subsequent heads of the School introduced any changes. Besides laying down the doctrines Epicurus organised the School on humane and practical lines. No stated fee was required from its members; each contributed according to his means and inclination. Membership was open to all classes of society, including slaves, without distinction of age or sex. There was no entrance requirement apart from basic literacy.

A striking and novel feature of the organisation was the pledge of personal loyalty to Epicurus which all adherents were required to give in the form: 'I will be faithful to Epicurus in accordance with whom I have made it my choice to live.' One is reminded here of the organisation of early Christian communities, and the similarity is further confirmed by Epicurus's practice of organising 'cells' of followers in other cities, with contact maintained by letter. We hear of Letters addressed to the 'friends' at Lampsacus, in Egypt, in Asia, and so on. Epicurus wanted to substitute friendliness for coercion as the binding force in human society. Perhaps he put too much trust in the 'milk of human kindness'. Cicero thought he did, vigorously repudiating the Epicurean approach as dangerously subversive of law and order. In general the School incurred much ill-informed criticism, and indeed odium. They were accused of atheism and unbridled pleasure-seeking. Seneca, however, knew better, and paid a striking tribute to the essentially refined morality of its genuine devotees.

The Athenians were proud of Epicurus and set up a statue of him. All our sources agree that he was a man of great kindliness and humanity, who lived in a modest and self-controlled way, delighting in the company of friends. There is a touch of nobility, and even saintliness, in his last recorded words. Though dying in great agony from a urinary obstruction he was able to write to his friend Idomeneus that he was persevering in contentment to the end: 'I have a bulwark against all this pain from the joy in my soul at the memory of our conversations together.'

The principal doctrines of Epicurus

(A) Physics and cosmology

Epicurus accepted the atomic theory of Democritus as the true basis for explaining the world of objects that we perceive through the senses. Despite his emphasis on sensation as the foundation of knowledge he thus accepted a way of ordering experience which was based on the demands of reason rather than the findings of perception. Neither atoms nor empty space could be perceived by the senses, but there were, he thought, a number of convincing reasons for inferring their existence. For example, we cannot see the wind, but it has the power to stir up the sea and blow down trees, so it must consist of a stream of invisible bodies that make an impact on the visible ones. Empty space cannot be perceived either, but its existence is required to explain certain facts such as the percolation of water through rocks or the passage of sound through the walls of houses.

He pointed out that indestructible atoms provide a permanent basis for change. Things do not finally disappear. They are simply resolved back into their basic parts. If this were not so there would be no limit to destruction, and in fact everything in the world would by now have vanished. The permanent stock of atoms provides a residual reservoir of material from which new things are constantly being formed. The atoms are the 'generative seeds' of things, and no species of plant or animal can come into existence unless the appropriate kinds of atoms pre-exist in the appropriate place and come together at the right time.

In cosmology he took the view that before our world was formed the atoms composing it were streaming rapidly downwards through the infinite expanse of empty space, moving without plan or purpose. Democritus thought that atoms were weightless, and that they moved in all directions. Epicurus modified the theory at this point by attributing various degrees of weight to the atoms, and picturing their weight as carrying them downwards in straight lines with the rapidity of thought. This made it difficult to see how they could collide and interlock to form larger bodies.

To overcome this difficulty Epicurus introduced a further notable modification into the Democritean theory. He supposed that from time to time an individual atom would spontaneously deviate by the smallest possible amount from its straight line path. This was

141

the somewhat notorious hypothesis of the *clinamen*, or 'atomic swerve', for which no evidence was offered or explanation given. But on the supposition that it occurred Epicurus was able to explain how composite bodies came into existence. The spontaneous swerving of individual atoms caused collisions and re-bounds, and set up a tangle of criss-cross motions, as a result of which atoms became bonded and hooked together to form the larger visible masses which we call sky, air, earth, and sea. The sky was viewed as a sort of container or envelope separating off our world from infinite space, and within it further aggregations of the atoms led to the successive development of plants and animals. Some of the early animals were monstrous, ill-adapted creatures which were unable to survive and propagate their species. Epicurus developed a view not unlike the Darwinian hypothesis of the 'survival of the fittest' to account for the apparent purposiveness in organic adaptations.

Epicurus was at pains to rule out any divine intervention in the process of world formation. He was not an atheist, for he accepted that gods did exist. But he located the gods outside the world, and in the spaces between the worlds. Our world was not in his view the only world. Given the infinite number of atoms and the boundless extent of void, one had to accept that other worlds had also come fortuitously into existence in other parts of space. But the gods were not interested in our world, or in any world, and they did not intervene in any natural process. Natural processes had natural explanations. This was the great Epicurean shield against the superstitious awe and fear of the gods which was regarded as casting a dark shadow over human life. Lucretius speaks in glowing terms of the great Greek intellectual achievement in raising human eyes to survey the heavens without fear, and in breaking out through the 'flaming walls of the world' to contemplate and comprehend the true nature of matter and space. Epicurus in his eyes was the main-spring of this achievement in that he gathered up all the previous advances and wove them together into a coherent system whose comprehension made man the equal of the gods in untroubled understanding and felicity.

(B) Doctrine of soul
Epicurean psychology is an elaborate off-shoot of Epicurean physics. In order to complete his victory over superstition, Epicurus gave a materialistic explanation of the soul which denied it immor-

tality. He conceived of soul-matter as composed of very small, fine-textured atoms, spherical in shape, which could be set in rapid motion by the slightest impact. These soul atoms he thought, were of four different kinds: wind-atoms, heat-atoms, air-atoms, and a nameless atomic component responsible for sensation (equivalent to the electrical energy of the nervous system in our terminology). The unnamed component was made up of the smallest and smoothest atoms of all, and is the first to be set in motion by external stimuli. Its motions constitute perceptions, and if, for example, they constitute a perception of impending danger, they are caught up by the heat element in the body. Then by the unseen energy of the wind- and air-atoms, the blood is quickened, the pupils of the eye dilate, and all parts of the body are roused to appropriate movement.

The Lucretian account of the doctrine emphasises the close and intimate connection between soul-matter and body-matter. They are 'interlocked by common roots and cannot easily be torn apart'. It is only when they are together that movement and sentience become possible, and that life is generated. Neither perceives apart from the other, and when they are parted at death the body soon decays and breaks down into its constituent atoms.

Soul was viewed in materialistic terms as a *part* of our corporeal make-up, and just as truly a part as hand or foot or eye. When faced with the problem of explaining the dominant or controlling force of 'mind' as distinct from matter Epicurus drew a distinction within soul-matter between 'mind' (in Latin *animus*) and 'vital-spirit' (in Latin *anima*). The *animus*, or mind, was composed of atoms of wind and heat, and was concentrated in the mid-region of the breast, where we feel the pulse of fear and the 'caressing touch of joy'. The *anima*, or vital spirit, though essential for the processes of life, was less dominant because it was more diffused through the trunk and limbs. In the normally functioning organism the 'mind' element passed on impulses to the 'vital-spirit' element, which moved under its direction and in turn moved the limbs. Normally the operation of the mind is not directly apparent, but if the mind itself is put into violent motion, for example, by an overwhelming fear, its perturbations have visible effects throughout the body in sweating, pallor, trembling limbs, buzzing ears, and so on. Epicurus understood these effects as motions directly communicated from the mind-element to the body by contact, and this was an additional confirmation that the mind is as material as the body. Conversely the 'nerve-racking impact' of a spear was transmitted into the mind-element as a shattering vibration.

Neither mind nor vital spirit is immortal. Both are born and both die. At birth the fine smooth atoms of which they are composed are gathered together in the envelope of the body. At death they are scattered and dispersed like water flowing out of a broken vessel. Epicurus argued cleverly against the notion of transmigration. If that doctrine were true we might find brave deer or cowardly lions! The soul is not inserted into the body from outside. It grows in intimate connection with it, forming such a close union that even our teeth share in sensation. This intimate association of soul and body makes it impossible for either to exist without the other. Death must therefore be understood as the dissolution of both. 'When we are, death is not; when death is, we are not.' He regarded this as a scientific fact with a most important bearing on the nature and conduct of life.

(C) Ethics

Epicurus's doctrine of pleasure was the most novel and distinctive feature of his ethical thought. Plato had depreciated pleasure, regarding its pursuit as inconsistent with the acquisition of virtue. This puritan attitude stemmed from his tendency to regard soul and body as two separate entities, with man's higher nature concentrated in an immaterial soul, and pleasure a bodily phenomenon. Aristotle regarded soul as inextricably linked with body in a form–matter relationship. Consequently he took a more positive view of pleasure, regarding it as psychical rather than physical, and as an important component of general well-being. It was not, however, in his view, an end in itself, but something which manifested itself in the wake of activity when that activity was unimpeded. He gave a number of good reasons for associating pleasure very closely with activity, and concluded that in general pleasure is a perfection that supervenes on activity when the conditions of that activity are favourable.

Epicurus went even further than Aristotle in his reaction against Plato's distrust of pleasure. He maintained that the true end and goal of human life is the maximisation of pleasure. He made the common-sense observation that all animals avoid pain, and from that he drew the simple inference that everyone should aim at

pleasure. Inevitably this ethical hedonism was popularly misin-
terpreted as a licence for unlimited self-indulgence, and the Epicureans got a bad name as reckless libertines. But Epicurus was
careful to fence his pleasure principle with the qualifications necessary to ensure that it could become a reputable rule of life. 'Every
pleasure', he said, 'is in itself good, but not all are to be chosen.' We
should not necessarily seek the pleasure of the moment. Reckless
enjoyment of pleasure may be followed by pain that more than
outweighs the pleasure. We need a hedonic calculus. Our aim
should be to get a credit balance of pleasure taken over the whole of
life from cradle to grave. This, he argued, was the rational way to
pursue pleasure. Beyond a certain point (when all painful wants
have been removed) pleasures can only be varied, not heightened.
A discriminating person will see that certain pleasures are more
durable than others of a more intense but more short-lived kind. By
investing in the quieter and more prolonged pleasures, which
Epicurus called 'static' as opposed to 'kinetic', one could best
ensure the psychological well-being and mental tranquillity essential for happy living.

'Static' pleasures were particularly associated with mental activity, including memory and hope. And here Epicurus recommended
the study of philosophy as the least stressful and most rewarding
form of mental activity. In particular, if one followed the Epicurean
system one would be immunised against the fear of the supernatural
which he regarded as the most potent destroyer of mental tranquillity. Fear of the dark, fear of ghosts, fear of death, fear of hell — all
these he considered to be childish and irrational phobias which
must be duly exorcised by his philosophy. He regarded the doctrine
of the mortality of the soul, and the doctrine of the non-interference
of the gods in human affairs or natural processes, as the main
bulwarks against the mental unease and anguish which he saw
pervading society. The philosopher must reason himself out of such
fears and anxieties, and he can then proceed to maximise his
enjoyment of life on the basis of self-control, self-improvement,
tolerant attitudes, and the cultivation of like-minded and congenial
friends.

In practice, Epicurus agreed with the Stoics in commending the
traditional cardinal virtues, but he did so from a different theoretical stand-point. For the Stoics they were expressions of the rational
in conduct, for Epicurus a tried and tested way to maximise plea-

sure. He said: 'One cannot live pleasantly without living wisely, honourably, and justly; nor can one live wisely, honourably, and justly, without living pleasantly.' Wisdom enabled one to make an appropriate selection of pleasurable activities. Temperance was the avoidance of intense but transient pleasures. Fortitude was seen in the consistent rejection of groundless fears. Justice he prized, though he regarded it as having a conventional rather than a natural basis. He adopted the social contract view of justice, regarding it as a matter of enlightened self-interest that human beings should agree to abstain from harming or injuring one another on the basis of 'do as you would be done by'. Justice is, or should be, a set of rules formed to adjust conflicting interests and geared to produce the maximum of pleasure for all members of a social group.

(D) Epicurus and society

Epicurus rejected the Stoic belief that human society is an expression of universal mind, and that the community of rational beings forms an organic whole. On the contrary, he regarded the state as an external association of individuals for mutual help and protection. The individual had no fundamental obligation to contribute to public life. He pointed out that many public figures become the targets of derision, abuse, and even hatred. To be in the public eye is to be in a potentially stressful situation. Hence the Epicurean doctrine of quietism, with its watchword: 'Live unobtrusively'. One should not go into politics unless one's nature was so restless that one could not find happiness in the seclusion of private life. Seneca puts it neatly: 'According to Zeno the sage will go into public life unless something occurs to prevent him. According to Epicurus the sage will not go into public life unless something occurs to compel him.'

It might be held against Epicurus that society would collapse if everyone opted out in the prudential way that he recommends. And this feeling that his quietism went too far tends to be confirmed when one reads that he thought that perhaps the wise man should forego marriage and children as an estate more productive of disturbance than peace of mind. At least it was an honest rather than a cynical expression of opinion. He does not seem to have been strongly anti-family, for he is reported as having been generous to his brothers and on good terms with his parents. And he was certainly not anti-social in his doctrine of friendship as the greatest single factor making for happiness. Epicurus was no wild libertine, but a sane and perceptive person who was much loved by his associates. Following his example, his School always set great store by friendship. Horace was not a consistent follower, but he had his Epicurean moments, and he well summed up the doctrine of friendship in his line: 'I judge soundly when I value a pleasant friend as the best of possessions.'

Religious observance is clearly an important aspect of social organisation. Epicurus was impressed by the wide diffusion of a belief in gods, and concluded that gods do exist, 'for the knowledge of them is clear'. What in his view was not clearly grasped was the nature of the gods and how they should be worshipped. He denied the truth of the popular picture of them and their activities, a picture which was reinforced by the poets. This, he thought, was a corrupted image. 'The impious man', he said, 'is not he who abolishes the gods of the multitude, but he who attaches the opinions of the multitude to the gods.' These benighted opinions included belief that the gods intervened in human affairs, that they could be influenced towards helping, or dissuaded from harming, human designs by prayers and offerings, and that their future intentions could be ascertained through omens or other forms of divination. Given the actual nature of the world, and the total detachment of the gods from it, such beliefs had to be regarded as the erroneous product of fear and ignorance. He rejected the case for divine providence, and said there was no point in supplicating the gods, and no means of ascertaining the future.

His attack on religion was not, however, total. He did recommend a practice that could be regarded as a form of worship. This was the contemplation of the perfection of the gods as realised in their indestructible nature as eternally living beings. He pictured the gods as leading a blissful way of life in detached tranquillity and friendly and intellectual converse with one another. In this way they provided the perfect model for happy human living, as Epicurus conceived it, and the contemplation of them would assist human endeavour towards this ideal. This was the refined and purified form of religion which he offered his followers. If visible images of them were required as an aid to contemplation, he recommended that they should be depicted with smiles on their faces, and not in the threatening guises of the popular art tradition.

Meditation on the divine nature was recommended by Epicurus

as an important and positive therapeutic technique for ridding the soul of anxiety and achieving blissful tranquillity of spirit. It was the first point in a scheme of precepts known as the *Tetrapharmakon*, or 'fourfold remedy', for human misery and discontent. The second point was to have a right attitude to death as the final dissolution of soul and body, putting an end to any further possibility of thought or feeling. As such, death was simply and totally irrelevant to the human condition, and acceptance of the mortality of the soul ensured against any fear of underworld punishment. The third point involved acceptance of a simple and frugal regime as the basis for healthy, pleasant living. Some pain and sickness were unavoidable, but if these were slight they were bearable, and if severe they did not last long. In general he urged that the necessities of life are easily procured, and that once the means to counter deprivations like cold and hunger have been secured, bodily pleasure is quickly felt, and is not enhanced by the addition of superfluous luxuries. Business competition to secure such luxuries is not worth the trouble it causes, and one should accustom oneself to do without them by living in the simplest possible way. Epicurus himself is quoted as saying that if he had bread and water he would vie with Zeus in happiness. The fourth point emphasised the extreme desirability of repose of mind, which could best be obtained through study of the Epicurean system of philosophy, and discussion of it with congenial friends.

Epicureanism was not a heroic creed, but it was a far from ignoble one. Despite misrepresentation and abuse it gained many adherents and survived for many centuries because of its inherent humanity, tolerance, and good sense.

THE SCEPTICS

Background
Like Stoicism and Epicureanism, Scepticism took shape as a coherent philosophical system at the beginning of the Hellenistic age, but it was not an entirely new phenomenon. Some strong sceptical trends had already appeared in Greek thought from Zeno onwards.

The term 'sceptic' (*skeptikos**) means by derivation a 'considerer' or 'examiner', and the Sceptics were thinkers who adopted a detached and critical attitude to all received opinions and doctrines.

148

Critical attitudes are not necessarily inconsistent with the holding of positive views, as the examples of Plato and Aristotle show. But in the history of philosophy periods of dogmatism and system-building tend to be succeeded by periods of radical and destructive re-appraisal, especially when great social and political changes are also taking place. The early Hellenistic age was just such a period. Previous philosophical reflection had generated as much doubt as certainty, and the various strains of doubt now gained added force in the inevitable reaction against Platonism and Aristotelianism, and also against the new ethical systems. There was obviously such a contrast between the world-views of Stoicism and Epicureanism that both could not be true, and this raised the possibility that neither was true. If one did not wish to exert oneself to make a choice between them, one could always take up a neutral stance by suspending judgement in relation to the truth of either, and affirming that dogmatic certainty was unattainable, and this was the course taken by the early Sceptics.

Early Scepticism: Pyrrho and his School

Pyrrho of Elis (*c*.365/360–*c*.275/270) is regarded as the first Greek to have formulated and taught a considered scepticism. He has left us no writings, but the names of some of his pupils are known, and it seems that his School continued in existence for a generation or so after his death. Scepticism as a philosophical system was then taken over by the 'New' Academy.

Pyrrhonian Scepticism was essentially a technique for achieving the mental imperturbability which all the Hellenistic Schools agreed in regarding as the basis for contented living. A report of the views of Pyrrho's pupil Timon of Phlius (*c*.320–230) will serve as a starting point for outlining the system.

Timon said that anyone who wanted to live contentedly must think seriously about three questions: (1) What is the nature of things? (2) How ought we to react to things? (3) What is the gain for those who have so reacted?

The Sceptical answers to these key questions were clear and consistent. The Pyrrhonians held that contradictory judgements may always be made about things, and there is no way of determining which judgement is true. As a result we can have no certain knowledge about the nature of things (1). We ought to react to them by suspending judgement, and by not committing ourselves to any definite statement about them (2). The practical consequence of this reaction will be a lack of any passionate involvement with things or strong desire for them, since we do not know what we may actually be desiring. The Sceptic becomes a detached observer, regarding the changing appearances of things with unruffled tranquillity (3). This was held to be the great practical benefit to be derived from the philosophical position, though others might regard it as an unacceptable relapse into apathy. Pyrrho's 'indifference' is illustrated by his saying that 'it makes no difference whether one is alive or dead'. In practice the Sceptics relaxed the full rigour of their indifference principle by making choices according to custom in the daily round of life. It was told of Pyrrho that he apologised for becoming agitated when attacked by a fierce dog, saying that it was hard to lay aside humanity completely!

Scepticism in the Academy: Arcesilaus and Carneades

Arcesilaus (315–241) became head of the Academy towards the middle of the third century, and steered it towards Sceptical views. He commended suspension of judgement, but not just as a play-safe mental attitude. He considered it to be a reputable philosophic position, inherent in the undogmatic attitude of Socrates, and acceptable also, he thought, to Plato. Platonism certainly furnished strong arguments against the reliability of the senses, and these were used as polemical ammunition against the dogmatic sensationalism of the Stoics and Epicureans. If the basis of their epistemology was suspect, it followed that one could have no confidence in the superstructure. So far from comprehension arising from clear perceptions, as Zeno taught (see above, pp.133-34), the only outcome of perceptual awareness had to be a lack of comprehension of the real nature of external objects.

The polemical side of Scepticism was strongly developed in the New Academy, and Arcesilaus is said to have devoted all his lectures to the refutation of other people's views. He made Scepticism the official outlook of the Academy, and this trend continued under Carneades (214–129), whose main contribution was to develop a theory of probability as a guide to action. This theory assessed the 'presentations' derived from the senses, and graded them according to their plausibility or persuasiveness. The more plausible a presentation the greater the likelihood that it was true in the sense of corresponding to reality. When choices or decisions had

150

to be made, Carneades held that one should rely on the most plausible or probable of the appearances as one's guide in action.

Later Scepticism

The Academy continued to be a centre of Scepticism until the headship of Antiochus of Ascalon in the decade 80–70. Outside its walls, Pyrrhonism was revived by Aenesidemus (*fl.c.*50) and others, who systematised the arguments against the possibility of acquiring knowledge, setting them out in text-book form in a series of 'tropes' or 'moves' which could be used to counter all assertions of the reliability of the senses or the validity of knowledge. The tropes were partly logical in form, and partly drawn from the illusory and contradictory nature of sensible appearances. The logical tropes denied that it was possible to discover self-evident axioms or construct deductively certain proofs. The others attempted to erect an insurmountable barrier between appearance and reality. For example, it was pointed out that rugged mountains seen at a distance look smooth, a square tower looks round, and so on. It was also pointed out that sensible objects present different appearances to the different senses, and that these appearances can vary according to the context in which the object is perceived and the emotional or physical state of the perceiver. Older sophistical arguments were also recalled relating to the relativity of customs and morals. The upshot of all these various types of argument was to stress the subjective nature of perceptions and ideas, and to indicate that we can never be sure that we have reliable and objective knowledge about the nature of the external world. Scepticism as a tradition of sustained and systematic doubt is extensively reported in the extant books of the sceptical physician Sextus Empiricus (*fl.c.*AD200), who is a principal source for the whole movement.

11

PLOTINUS AND NEOPLATONISM

THE CHARACTER OF Plotinus (AD204–270) is vividly portrayed in
an extant biography by his pupil Porphyry, who tells us that his
master refused to talk about his origins, and that he would never
allow his birthday to be celebrated, nor his portrait to be painted.
As a philosophical idealist he presumably considered such triv-
ialities unworthy of record. We can be reasonably sure that Greek
was his native language, but there is uncertainty about his birth-
place. This may have been in Egypt, but the first certain fact about
him is that at the age of twenty-seven he went to study philosophy at
Alexandria. At first he found no teacher to his liking, but he was
then taken to hear Ammonius Saccas (*fl.c.*AD225), and after attend-
ing his lectures he exclaimed: 'This is the man I was looking for.'

He remained with Ammonius for eleven years, and then in 243 he
migrated to Rome. His name has a not un-Roman sound, and he
may have had connections with the Roman aristocracy — Trajan
had a wife called Plotina. At all events he began to teach philosophy
at Rome, and by 263, when Porphyry joined his school, he was a
well-established figure with an influential circle of friends and
disciples.

Plotinus was an idealistic thinker who believed he could give
positive answers to the great philosophical questions about God, the
soul, and the world. Looking back over the whole course of Greek
philosophy he tried to distill its inherited wisdom into one all-
embracing and spiritualistic system. Plotinus did not call himself a
Neoplatonist, which is a term that modern historians have devised
for him and his followers. He regarded himself as an orthodox
Platonist. Plato the 'divine' philosopher was his supreme authority,
standing high above criticism.

The senior member of his school, a devout man called Amelius, once asked Plotinus to accompany him to a temple sacrifice. Plotinus replied enigmatically: 'It is for them to come to me, not me to them.' It seems that for Plotinus the externals of worship held no great interest or importance. He was not actively hostile to cult — just indifferent. Religion for him was an intensely personal affair, an inward experience of the divine presence, not a matter of external observance or ceremony. There is no evidence that he ever had any close contact with orthodox Christians, but he was bitterly opposed to the Gnostics, a group of theosophical sectaries who flourished during the early centuries of our era on the mystical interface between Judaism, Christianity, and Mithraism. One major point of difference was that the Gnostics believed in the existence of an evil world-soul, or devil, while the Neoplatonists refused to allow that there was any evil element in the spiritual realm.

The other-worldliness of Plotinus's outlook was strongly marked. During his lifetime the Roman Empire was often in turmoil and suffered many misfortunes, but there is no hint of this in his writings. Yet at the same time he was noted for his ability to give practical advice to his friends. The persons and property of orphaned children were not seldom entrusted to his care, and he discharged the duties of guardianship with scrupulous attention to their welfare. Once, when Porphyry was in a suicidal mood, Plotinus told him that his wish to take his life was not a rational decision, but due to an excess of black bile, and ordered him away for a rest and change of air. This was the last that Porphyry saw of his master, for he died soon afterwards on a friend's estate near Naples. His school broke up after his death, but his thought continued to exercise great influence.

His last recorded utterance, addressed on his death-bed to his friend Eustochius, was: 'Try to bring back the god in you to the Divine in the All.' This pregnant saying encapsulates the mysticism which was a leavening element in his thought. He inherited and worked within the best traditions of Greek rationalism deriving ultimately from Plato and Pythagoras. But he was also a mystic in the sense that his philosophy was enhanced and deepened in its spirituality by a recurrent experience of mystical union with the divine nature. His mysticism helped him to re-think the elements of Platonism in such a way that he transmuted them into what was virtually a new system. This is the justification for the label of

Neoplatonism. Plotinus did not intend to be a revolutionary, but because of his genius for original philosophising he was able to produce a vital and coherent system which totally superseded the somewhat ramshackle constructions of his immediate predecessors.

Writings

Plotinus did not start to write until his fiftieth year. From then on until his death sixteen years later he produced a steady stream of short treatises on various aspects of his system. These writings were not intended for general publication, but only for circulation among his friends and pupils. They were not planned as a single work, and can stand as separate essays, but each presupposes the whole system, which had already taken firm shape in Plotinus's mind.

Plotinus asked Porphyry to undertake the task of editing these essays, and this he conscientiously did, collecting and arranging them in six books. The edition eventually appeared thirty years after Plotinus's death. It contained fifty-four essays arranged roughly according to subject matter in *'enneads'*, or 'groups of nine', and *Enneads* is the title which the collection still bears.

The *Enneads* are written in a terse but rich style, and each essay, like a good sermon, is aimed directly at the reader's perplexities and his moral improvement. Passages of very tough argument alternate with sections of sublime eloquence. The Greek is far from easy, but never deliberately obscure. The work has been well called 'an ever renewed intelligent struggle to express the inexpressible'.

The system

(A) The One or the Good

Plotinus held that when human beings are awakened and recalled to their true selves by the practice of philosophy, they can rise to a universality of thought which is all-comprehending. But at this point they come to realise the truth of the paradox first hinted at by Plato that the ultimate ground of reality lies 'above and beyond reality'. Since this prime source of existence transcends existence, any attempted description must fail to do justice to it, and will limit and determine unacceptably what is by nature ineffable.

But despite the logical impossibility of characterising it in any way, Plotinus does venture to use two names to designate and refer to his ultimate first principle. He sometimes calls it the One. But his preferred name, following Plato's usage in the *Republic*, is the Good. This designation reminds us that the first principle of reality is not negative, but supremely positive. The Good is the ground of all values. It is a Goodness which is so rich and full that it *overflows* to generate the world of the Intellect and the lower levels of reality derived therefrom. It is also a Goodness so lovely and desirable that it draws back towards itself all that has flowed out from itself. This transcendent source of existence and value is Deity *par excellence*, and to come into Its presence and be united with It in contemplative ecstasy is the supreme goal of intellectual and spiritual aspiration.

(B) The first emanation from the One/Good:
the World-Mind or Intellect

One of Plotinus's chosen terms for expressing the spontaneous overflowing of the One/Good is *emanation*. The first product of its creative activity is the World-Mind, or Intellect, which emanates from its divine source like water welling out from a perennial spring, or like light radiating from the sun. The source is in no way diminished by these out-pourings because it is inexhaustible — a superabundant reservoir of existence and life. The overflowing is necessary because, given the nature of the Good, it cannot be conceived as not happening. It is also a spontaneous out-pouring because it does not happen under any constraint. And finally it is a never-ending out-pouring because the source is eternally active. The creativity of the Good is not something that called the universe into existence at some remote time in the past, and then left it to its own devices. The emanation of derived being is not intermittent but continuous.

So the first aspect of the timeless formation of the world is the endless out-pouring of an indescribable vitality that springs from the ultimate source of all being. Plotinus calls it 'vision that has not yet achieved sight'. As incipient seeing it immediately turns back to view the One from which is has proceeded, but it fails to regain the One in its primal unity. Instead it 'breaks up' and 'makes itself many', like the jet of a fountain falling back on itself in countless drops of spray. A jet of water constantly becomes many, yet retains a unity of form, so long as the fountain plays. In the same way the world of Intellect as the first emanation from the One combines an

155

out-going multiplicity of form with a dynamic inner unity of structure.

(C) The second emanation: the World-Soul

The World-Soul emanates from Intellect in a way closely parallel to the emanation of Intellect from the One, and constitutes the third member of a closely linked trio of Substances. Plotinus calls them 'God', 'second God', and 'third God' respectively. Some might be tempted to draw a parallel with the Christian doctrine of the Trinity. But this would be a mistake, because the Substances are not co-equal, but the substance which emanates is subordinate to the substance from which it is derived.

This notion of subordination forms a key aspect of Plotinus's distinctive theory of causality. The different levels of reality represented by the successive emanations are not to be thought of as appearing one after the other in a time sequence, but rather as standing in a timeless relationship of superiority and dependence. The relationship is causally one-sided because the higher level produces and determines the lower without losing anything of its superior perfection. The lower level is inevitably inferior in its essential being, because a superior cause can never be totally and perfectly reflected in its effect. But a being on a lower level can redeem itself from its imperfections by recognising and identifying itself with its cause.

The World-Soul is the universal principle of Life, including all individual souls within its essence. Plotinus compares it to a 'radius from a centre', at once 'attached to the Supreme', and yet reaching down into the sphere of body. Soul can live in the world of the Intellect, and can rise with Intellect to transcend itself and merge with the One. It can also live in the sensible world where it is responsible for perception, and for the formation and ordering of material bodies. No matter at what level it is functioning, the One and the Intellect are always present to it and acting upon it. Intellect, by illuminating individual souls, raises them towards its own level, and if they respond fully they are ultimately drawn into union with the One or Good.

World-Soul, however, more than World-Mind, shows a certain 'wilfulness' in its desire to be independent and live its own life, and this wilfulness of Soul is, for Plotinus, the origin of the temporal world. The World-Mind operates in such a way that it has complete and simultaneous knowledge of all possible objects of thought. Its mode of living is an eternal mode in which there is nothing but repose and stability. If the World-Soul shares in this life it merges with the World-Mind. It can only assert its independence and difference from Intellect by living a life in which there is succession, movement, and change. The World-Soul's wilfulness shows itself in a sort of restless desire for passing on from one thing to another. Because it apprehends objects successively, it in effect creates Time, which is born out of the self-transforming life of Soul, as it moves on from one mode of living to another. The objects successively apprehended by the World-Soul are also apprehended in separation from one another, and this apprehension gives them a spatial as well as a temporal framework. So the World-Soul produces Space as well as Time by its contemplative activity.

(D) The third emanation: the material universe or world of nature
The material universe comes into existence in the Space-Time created by the World-Soul. Its growth is compared by Plotinus to that of a seed, which, as it grows larger, 'dissipates its intrinsic unity', and 'goes forward to a weaker extension'. In this extended world mass the life of the World-Soul expresses itself in continuous movement, through which it infuses design and system into matter from within. This ordering of the material world is done by Soul with the aid of *logoi* which it receives from Intellect, and which it embodies in things as it makes them. The *logoi* are active formative principles derived from the higher reaches of reality. With their aid Soul keeps the material universe in the best order of which it is capable, and unifies it in so far as what is in space and time can be unified.

We tend to think of souls as contained in bodies. Plotinus has the magnificent conception of all bodies as contained in the boundless ocean of Soul. The world of nature is brilliantly compared to a net floating in the all-encompassing medium of the spiritual world, 'immersed in life, but unable to appropriate the element in which it swims. The net spreads out as far as it can in the sea, which is already spread out.'

(E) Matter
The line of emanation and descent from the One ends in the utter negativity and formlessness of Matter, which is the final end-

product of the progressive outward and downward movement of things away from Unity and Goodness. Matter has no positive or determinate existence. It is the passive receptacle of sensible Forms, a kind of medium in which they are present 'like reflections in an invisible and formless mirror'. Because of its utter negativity the last and limiting matter of the sensible world is so far removed from the Good that it must be regarded as evil. It should not be able to affect bodies which are informed by Soul, but somehow it seems to infect them with something of its own darkness or emptiness. Matter imparts a certain defect to things, making them less real and good than they should be.

The task of philosophy
Philosophising in the Plotinian mode is only possible for those who accept and share certain basic beliefs about the nature of reality. One must believe in the existence of an invisible world of intelligible being that far transcends the visible material world in significance and value. One must also believe in the 'divinity' of the soul. Plotinus holds that each human soul is 'divine', in the sense that its existence is ultimately derived from the supreme source of all reality. But he also thought that this basic relationship of kinship between man and God is inevitably distorted and weakened by the conditions of human life. The task of philosophy is to restore the relationship to its full strength and significance. It does this by re-awakening us to a knowledge of our true self and its place in the scheme of reality. 'If you marvel at the world,' he said, 'marvel at your own soul.' He held that we cannot fully know ourselves except in our cosmic context, and the most fundamental thing in this context is our soul's relationship with the Divine All, by which he meant the world of intelligible being, together with its source, the Good or the One.

Every soul, he believed, has at least a vague impulse to seek a return to its divine source, and this impulse lies at the core of our nature, and is the root of all religion. The impulse is not just an idle or gratuitous whim. It constitutes the very ground of our existence as individual persons. The function of philosophy is to lend wings to this impulse, helping us to concentrate our awareness of ourselves in such a way that we can progress upwards towards a closer union with the ultimate Good.

Philosophy shows us how to become what we essentially are — a paradox which lies at the heart of idealism. As such, philosophy functions as a religion, helping the soul to return to its Maker. It is not surprising that in the fifth and sixth centuries AD the Neoplatonist philosophy contributed significantly to the formation of Christian theology.

Plotinus accepted that the everyday world is far from perfect, but he also protested against the pessimistic Gnostic view of the world as intrinsically bad throughout. In one passage he describes the world as 'a fine clear image of the intelligible gods'. He insists that anyone who despises and hates the visible world, and who finds no beauty in it, cannot really come to know and love the beauty of the intelligible world.

He also responded much more favourably than Plato to the beauty inherent in works of art. For Plato a work of art was a copy of a copy, 'twice removed from reality', and the artist little better than a conjuror or illusionist. Plotinus took a higher view of the artist as one who imitates God in imposing form on matter. In his view the essence of beauty is the domination of matter by form. The artist must try to comprehend the rational formative principles from which natural objects are derived. He must have some grasp of the unifying power of symmetry, order, and proportion, and he must seek to embody these elements in his work. In so doing he draws something down from the higher world, and bodies it forth in the world of sense. How, he asks, did Phidias create his famous statue of Zeus at Olympia? He certainly did not copy a human model. Rather, he pondered on 'what form Zeus would take if he wished to appear to us in human shape'. This theory of 'images' as the reflection and embodiment of unseen spiritual realities became the basis and justification for Byzantine Christian art. But Beauty, in Plotinus's view, was something more than good proportion. He held that there is a vital quality about a great work of art which draws people to love and admire it. The artist of a masterpiece has managed to tap the ageless vitality of the unseen world of the spirit. We might paraphrase Keats, and say that for Plotinus: 'Beauty is life, life beauty.'

In summary then, Plotinus is recommending a right appreciation and use of the beauties of nature and art as a part of philosophic living, just as much as he exhorts people to self-discipline. Both are necessary preliminary steps on the upward path, but neither must be made an end in itself.

Conclusion

The Plotinian system confronts the human soul with a clear metaphysical choice. It can continue to drift downwards aimlessly on the path of self-will. Or it can choose the upward path of salvation through the moral and intellectual disciplines of philosophy. The upward path turns out to be a path of inward purification in which the soul turns away from all that is external to it, and concentrates inwards upon itself in thoughtful meditation. In this way it is enabled to communicate with, and grasp, reality, because the higher realities of Intellect and the One are actively present in every soul.

> If there is to be perception of what is thus present, we must turn the perceptive faculty inward and hold it to attention there. Hoping to hear a desired voice we let all others pass and are alert for the coming at last of that most welcome of sounds: so here, we must let the hearings of sense go by, save for sheer necessity, and keep the Soul's perception bright and quick to the sounds from above (translation MacKenna–Page).

The influence of the system flowed on strongly after Plotinus's death, and for nearly three centuries his successors contended against the rising tide of Christianity for the allegiance of the best minds of the civilised world. Porphyry (234–*c*.305) became an influential figure in his own right. His *Against the Christians* widened the rift between the two systems that had already begun to show in Plotinus's antipathy to the Gnostics.

The final phase of Neoplatonism as a teaching school with recognised adherents was appropriately centred in the Platonic Academy at Athens. Its leading representatives were Proclus (410–485) and Damascius. Proclus presided over the Academy with great learning and diligence, producing a large corpus of work, much of which is still extant. His most influential book was his *Elements of Theology*, which provided something not to be found in Plotinus — a concise and systematic presentation of the principles of Neoplatonic metaphysics.

Damascius was head of the Academy when it and the other Greek schools were closed by order of the Emperor Justinian in AD529, a date traditionally regarded as marking the historical termination of Greek philosophy, though not, of course, the end of its intellectual hold on the human mind.

Neoplatonism represents the last creative effulgence of the movement towards a philosophical understanding of the world which Thales had initiated some eleven centuries before the Justinian closure. The system is a powerful affirmation of an invisible world of Mind dominating and sustaining the material world. It contains a remarkable blend of rationalism, poetic imagery, and spiritual aspiration. To Aristotle's question 'What is Being?' Plotinus and his followers reply that ultimately It is Good or God, transcending all that is perceivable, and also all that is intelligible. This is the mystical crown of the system deriving from the personal experience of the founder. But the system as a whole was in no way taken on trust. All of its parts were discussed and articulated in a fully rational way. It provided a comprehensive and elevating account of God, the soul, and the world, and its 'theology' differed from Christianity in being grounded in reason rather than revelation.

If one looks back over Greek philosophy as a whole, one can say that all its exponents accepted the Socratic exhortation to 'follow the argument wherever it leads'. From first to last the Greek thinkers maintained an unwavering faith in the power of human reason to discover the truth of things. Even the Sceptics' rejection of certitude was based on rational argument. One of the chief glories of Greek philosophy is that it fostered the light of reason and rolled back the darkness of superstition and fear. But the rational approach did not always lead to agnosticism — far from it. As the subject developed, the main current of speculation set ever more strongly in the direction of a theistic, or pantheistic, interpretation of the world. Plato posited a transcendent 'Maker and Father of this universe'. Aristotle argued from transient matter up to pure Form, which is God. The Stoics, though technically materialists, took an ennobling view of the matter of the world as permeated and activated by Divine Reason. In the words of Paul, the Greek-speaking Jew from Tarsus, 'the invisible things of Him were clearly seen' by the best minds of Greece.

161

GLOSSARY

akousmata: 'things heard'. A term used in Pythagorean circles for a collection of pithy sayings and precepts venerated as part of the traditional teaching of Pythagoras.

apatheia: 'absence of passion or emotion'. A state of mind especially prized by the Stoics as enabling reason to take complete control of conduct.

apeiron: '(the) boundless', '(the) unlimited'. The term chosen by Anaximander to characterise the primal stuff of the universe.

archē: 'beginning'. The term was rendered in Latin as *principium*, hence 'principle'. Used for the original source or cause of things, whether material or spiritual.

askēsis: 'training'. An athletic term transferred to mental and moral discipline; hence the origin of 'asceticism'.

atomon (sōma): 'uncuttable (body)'. Perhaps the original term used by the 'atomists' for the basic particles of matter as they conceived them.

dialektikê: 'the art of conversation'. From Zeno on the term had special application to philosophical discussion and argument. Plato appropriated it for the particular form of reasoning which he recommended for the study of the ultimate nature of reality (that is, the Forms or Ideas). Hence the modern use of 'dialectic' in philosophical contexts.

doxai: 'opinions', particularly of the various schools of philosophy, and later of religious sects. A 'doxographer' is one who records philosophical opinions or beliefs. 'Orthodoxy' is 'correct belief'; 'heterodoxy' is 'other-than-correct belief'.

162

epistēmê: 'knowledge'. Hence 'epistemology' as the study of how knowledge is obtained and certified. The word was rendered in Latin by *scientia* (= 'science').

ēthika: 'things pertaining to character (= ēthos)', that is, matters discussed in the systematic study of conduct, hence the science of 'ethics'.

eudaimonia: 'well-being', 'happiness'. The ultimate goal of all the Greek ethical systems.

gĕnĕsis: 'becoming', 'coming into being'.

harmonia: 'fitting together', 'adjustment'. Originally applied to the art of the carpenter or shipwright. Later it came to denote the special adjustment of strings and pegs in a harp or lyre, and hence the musical 'harmony' produced by such an instrument.

histŏria: 'enquiry', 'investigation', especially as practised by early Ionian geographers and historians, and also the 'information' so acquired, and the 'written treatise' in which it was embodied. 'Natural history' is by derivation 'research into nature'.

homoiomereia: 'likeness of parts'. A technical term for the characteristics of matter as envisaged by Anaxagoras.

hūlê: literally 'wood', 'timber', hence any common or easily worked material, and so 'matter'.

hŭpothesis: 'proposal', 'supposition'. The word seems to have first acquired a technical sense in geometry, being used of the 'assumptions' employed in the solution of problems of geometrical construction. It was then transferred to the 'premises' used in logical argument.

ĭdĕā: 'shape', 'form', originally used of the 'appearance' of a thing as grasped by sight, and then internalised, especially by Plato, to characterise the essential structure or invisible essence of an object. The Latin *species* shows a similar range of meanings. Modern senses of 'idea' have little or no relevance to the ancient meanings of the word.

kīnēsis: 'movement', 'change', hence 'kinetic' energy, and (c)inema (= 'movies').

kosmos: 'order'. Pythagoras may have been the first to apply the word to the 'world-order'; hence the '(orderly) universe'. The word certainly occurs in this sense in Heraclitus.

krĭtērion: 'standard of judgement', 'test of knowledge', used particularly for ways of assessing the validity of perceptions or feelings.

logos: literally 'statement', 'story', 'account'. The word acquired various specialised meanings, such as 'proportion' (in mathematics), and 'definition' (in philosophy). It was also used for a 'reason' or 'principle', and in later theology for the 'divine reason' manifest in the creation of the world. The root from which 'logic' is derived, and also all scientific terms ending in -logy, for example, biology, pathology, etc.

meta-phŭsika: literally 'things after the physical'. The term was originally applied to the treatise of Aristotle which (in the manuscript tradition) came after the *Physics*. Since this work dealt exclusively with abstract concepts such as cause and substance, this whole area of philosophy has come to be called 'metaphysics'.

philosophos: 'a lover of wisdom' (= *sophia*). Perhaps first used by Pythagoras to describe himself and his interests. A favourite word with Plato, often used in contrast with 'sophist'. Plato's conception of the aims and methods of 'philosophy' has coloured all subsequent uses of the term.

phusikos: 'a student of *phusis*'. A term used by Aristotle to describe the early Milesian thinkers.

phŭsis: 'nature'. What grows, or is there, as opposed to what is artificial or man-made. From Aristotle on the study of the 'physical' was delimited from the study of the 'metaphysical', and this has led to the modern usage of 'physics' as the scientific study of the material world.

psuchê: 'soul', sometimes viewed as the inherent life-principle of the body, and sometimes as a separate and immaterial entity capable of surviving death.

skeptikos: 'one who reflects and considers'. From the third century BC on the term tended to become narrowed to those whose reflections led them to doubt the possibility of acquiring any knowledge at all.

sophia, sophos: 'wisdom', 'wise'; also 'skill', 'skilled'. The terms were first used of any kind of expertise, but later tended to be restricted to good judgement in politics or morality.

sophistes: originally a practitioner of any skill, an adept, but from the middle of the fifth century BC restricted to educational experts or 'professors'. Plato contrasted 'sophists' with genuine seekers after knowledge, accusing them of misusing argument to bemuse and impress their pupils and the general public, and asserting that their pretended expertise was a sham. His strictures are largely responsible for the depreciatory sense now attached to the word 'sophistry'.

stoa: a 'covered colonnade' or 'portico'. The word 'Stoic' is derived from the 'Painted Porch' at Athens where Zeno used to lecture.

SUGGESTIONS FOR FURTHER READING

GENERAL HISTORIES

ARMSTRONG, A.H.: *An Introduction to Ancient Philosophy*, fourth edition, Methuen (University Paperbacks), London, 1972.

COPLESTON, F.C.: *A History of Philosophy*, Vol. 1, *Greece and Rome*, Burns and Oates, London, 1946; reprinted by Search, London, 1976.

DIOGENES LAERTIUS: *Lives of Eminent Philosophers*, two vols, in Greek, with parallel English translation by R.D. Hicks, Loeb Classical Library, Heinemann, London, and Putnam's, New York, 1925.

GUTHRIE, W.K.C.: *A History of Greek Philosophy*, six vols, Cambridge University Press, Cambridge, 1962–81. A very full and eminently sensible account. Carries the story down to Aristotle.

LONG, A.A.: *Hellenistic Philosophy*, second edition, Duckworth, London, 1968.

THE PRESOCRATICS

Texts

BARNES, J.: *Early Greek Philosophy*, Penguin Books Ltd, Harmondsworth, 1987. A fully representative selection of fragments and *testimonia* in English translation. A valuable aid for the student and beginner.

DIELS, H. and KRANZ, W.: *Die Fragmente der Vorsokratiker*, sixth edition, Lindemann and Ludecke, Berlin, 1951. An indispensable collection of the fragments in Greek, with relevant *testimonia*, for scholarly study.

FREEMAN, K.: *The Pre-Socratic Philosophers*, Blackwell, Oxford, 1946. An English translation of the fragments (but not the *testimonia*).

KIRK, G.S., RAVEN, J.E. and SCHOFIELD, M.: *The Presocratic Philosophers*, second edition, Cambridge University Press, Cambridge, 1983. A reasonably full selection of Greek texts (with English translations and critical commentary).

General works

ALLEN, R.E. and FURLEY, D.J. (EDS): *Studies in Presocratic Philosophy*, two vols, Routledge & Kegan Paul, London, 1970, 1975. An anthology of papers by leading authorities of the post-war period.

BARNES, J.: *The Presocratic Philosophers*, two vols, Routledge & Kegan Paul, London and Boston, 1979. Advanced, critical, sometimes unorthodox.

BURNET, J.: *Early Greek Philosophy*, fourth edition, Adam and Charles Black, 1945. A classic outline treatment.

CORNFORD, F.M.: *Principium Sapientiae*, Cambridge University Press, Cambridge, 1952. Evocative.

HUSSEY, E.: *The Presocratics*, Duckworth, London, 1972; reprinted, 1983. Nuanced and reliable.

PARTICULAR THINKERS

Presocratics

The Milesians
KAHN, C.H.: *Anaximander and the Origins of Greek Cosmology*, Columbia University Press, New York, 1960.

Pythagoras and the Pythagoreans
GUTHRIE, W.K.C.: *A History of Greek Philosophy*, Vol. 1. (See above, under General Histories.) The section on Pythagorean philosophy is virtually a book in itself.

Heraclitus
KAHN, C.H.: *The Art and Thought of Heraclitus*, Cambridge University Press, Cambridge, 1979.

Parmenides
GALLOP, D.: *Parmenides of Elea*, Toronto University, Toronto, 1984.

Anaxagoras
SCHOFIELD, M.: *An Essay on Anaxagoras,* Cambridge University Press, Cambridge, 1980.

The Atomists
BAILEY, C.: *The Greek Atomists and Epicurus,* Clarendon Press, Oxford, 1928; reprinted by Russell and Russell, New York, 1964.

The Sophists and Socrates

FERGUSON, J.: *Socrates: A Source Book,* Macmillan, London, 1970. A rich collection of materials.
GULLEY, N.: *The Philosophy of Socrates,* Macmillan, London, and St Martin's Press, New York, 1968.
GUTHRIE, W.K.C.: *A History of Greek Philosophy,* Vol. 3. (See above, under General Histories.) A very well-organised and detailed account, particularly good on the Sophists.
KERFERD, G.B.: *The Sophistic Movement,* Cambridge University Press, Cambridge, 1981.

Plato

The complete works in English
HAMILTON, E. and CAIRNS, H. (EDS): *The Collected Dialogues of Plato, Including the Letters,* Princeton University Press, Princeton, 1961; seventh printing, 1973. A handsome one-volume Plato with translations by a wide range of experts.
JOWETT, B.: *The Dialogues of Plato,* four vols, fourth edition, revised, edited by R.M. Hare, D.A. Russell, Sphere, London, 1970. A very stylish Victorian version, revised to take account of modern work, with new introductions to the dialogues.

General studies
ANNAS, J.: *An Introduction to Plato's Republic,* Clarendon Press, Oxford, 1981.
BRUMBAUGH, R.S.: *Plato for the Modern Age,* Crowell Collier, New York, 1962.
CROMBIE, I.M.: *An Examination of Plato's Doctrines,* two vols, Routledge & Kegan Paul, London, and Humanities Press, New York, 1963–9. Good exposition and penetrating criticism.
GRUBE, G.M.A.: *Plato's Thought,* Methuen, London, 1935. A sound introduction which has stood the test of time.

168

HARE, R.M.: *Plato*, Oxford University Press, Oxford and New York, 1982. A concise and elegant treatment in the Oxford *Past Masters* series.

RAVEN, J.E.: *Plato's Thought in the Making*, Cambridge University Press, Cambridge, 1965. An illuminating interpretation.

TAYLOR, A.E.: *Plato: The Man and His Work*, Methuen, London, 1926; seventh edition, 1971 (University Paperbacks). A classic treatment, containing lively analysis of the contents of all the major dialogues.

Aristotle

The complete works in English
ROSS, W.D. and SMITH, J.A. (EDS): *The Works of Aristotle Translated into English*, twelve vols, Clarendon Press, Oxford, 1908–52.

General studies
ACKRILL, J.L.: *Aristotle the Philosopher*, Oxford University Press, Oxford, 1981. Acute but sympathetic criticism.

BARNES, J.: *Aristotle*, Oxford University Press, Oxford and New York, 1982. A lively and trenchant addition to the *Past Masters* series.

LLOYD, G.E.R.: *Aristotle: The Growth and Structure of His Thought*, Cambridge University Press, Cambridge, 1968.

ROSS, W.D.: *Aristotle*, Methuen, London, 1923; fifth edition, revised, 1971. Comprehensive and authoritative.

THE HELLENISTIC SCHOOLS

Source material

ARNIM, VON, H.F.: *Stoicorum Veterum Fragmenta*, four vols, Leipzig 1903–24; reprinted, Stuttgart, 1964. Has long been the standard compilation of Stoic fragments.

LONG, A.A. and SEDLEY, D.N.: *The Hellenistic Philosophers*, two vols, Cambridge University Press, Cambridge, 1987. A comprehensive source-book. Vol. 1 contains the principal sources in English translation with philosophical commentary. Vol. 2 is an ancillary volume containing the Greek and Latin texts with notes and bibliography.

USENER, H.: *Epicurea,* Leipzig, 1887; reprinted, Stuttgart, 1966. Has long been the standard compilation of sources for Epicureanism.

General works

Stoicism

ARNOLD, E.V.: *Roman Stoicism,* Cambridge University Press, Cambridge, 1911; reprinted, Routledge & Kegan Paul, London, 1958. A classic treatment.

RIST, J.M.: *Stoic Philosophy,* Cambridge University Press, London, 1969.

SANDBACH, F.H.: *The Stoics,* Chatto and Windus, London, 1975.

WATSON, G.: *The Stoic Theory of Knowledge,* The Queen's University, Belfast, 1966.

Epicureanism

BAILEY, C.: *The Greek Atomists and Epicurus.* (See above, under The Atomists.)

FARRINGTON, B.: *The Faith of Epicurus,* Weidenfeld and Nicolson, London, 1967.

RIST, J.M.: *Epicurus: An Introduction,* Cambridge University Press, London, 1972.

Scepticism

SEXTUS EMPIRICUS: *Works,* four vols, in Greek, with parallel English translation by R.G. Bury, Loeb Classical Library, Heinemann, London, and Harvard University Press, Cambridge, Mass., 1935.

STOUGH, C.L.: *Greek Skepticism,* University of California, Berkeley, 1969.

NEOPLATONISM

PLOTINUS: *The Enneads,* translated by G.S. MacKenna, fourth edition, revised by B.S. Page, Faber, London, 1969. An outstanding translation, the product of a life-time's work.

WALLIS, R.T.: *Neoplatonism,* Duckworth, London, 1972.

INDEX

Academy, 11, 93, 96, 98, 101, 110, 149, 150-1, 160
agnosticism, 82
Air, element of, 23, 24, 27-9, 44, 60, 107-9, 119
Anaxagoras, 65-71; life, 65-7; influence, 71, 87, 116
Anaximander, 18, 22-7, 32, 46
Anaximenes, 18, 27-9, 32
Antiochus, of Ascalon, 151
apathy, 136, 150
appearance, and reality, 10, 51, 76-7, 84, 100
Arcesilaus, 150
Archelaus, 66, 71, 86
Archytas, 94, 95
argument, techniques of, 10; and Parmenides, 51-4; and Zeno, 56-8; and the Sophists, 81; and Socrates, 89-90; and the Sceptics, 151; *see also* dialectic, logic
Aristotle: and doxography, 14-15; and earlier thinkers, 20, 26, 28, 37, 43, 55, 57-8, 67, 73, 101; and Plato, 109, 110; in Academy, 110-11; life, 110-111; and the Lyceum, 111; writings, 111-14; philosophical method, 114-15, 129-30; on cause, 115-17; on universals, 117; on potentiality and actuality, 117-18; on matter and form, 118-19; on substance, 119-20; on world, 120-3; on God, 122-3; on happiness, 123-5; on moral excellence, 126-7; on intellectual excellence, 128-9; on pleasure, 144
astronomy, 10, 18, 19-20, 23, 29, 38-9, 93, 102, 106, 122
atheism, 84-5, 140
Athens, 65-6, 79, 80, 81, 84, 86, 87, 94, 96, 110, 132, 139
Atomism, atomic theory, 9, 10, 72-8, 120, 141-2

Babylonia, 18, 19, 21, 29, 38
beauty, 99, 100, 105, 159
books, early, 23, 25, 40-1, 81

Carneades, 150-1
cause: Plato on, 100; Aristotle on, 115-17, 120, 127; Plotinus on, 156; *see also* change, move-ment, world
change: and movement, 10, 22, 28; self-regulating, 25-6; through rarefaction and condensation, 28; like river, 45-6; denied by Parmenides, 51, 53; by mixture, 61; cyclical, 62-3; by movement of atoms, 74; Plato on, 109; Aristotle on, 117-18, 121-2; *see also* world process
Christianity, 93, 140, 153, 159, 160
cosmogony, 23-5; rejected, 44, 120; random, 142; *see also* world formation
cosmology, 23, 25-6, 62-4, 75-6, 107-9, 141-2; *see also* nature, world order, world process
cosmopolitanism, 66, 131-2, 137-8
cosmos, 37, 44, 107, 134-5; *see also* world order
Cratylus, 45, 48
creation: *ex nihilo* denied, 53, 62, 68; Plato on, 107-9; by the Good, 155; *see also* change, cosmogony, cosmology, destruction
Critias, 85, 88, 94
Cynic School, 93, 132

Damascius, 160
Democritus: life, 73; writings, 73; atomic theory, 74-5; cosmology, 75; epistemology, 76-7; and Epicurus, 141
destruction: absolute denied, 62, 68; of atomic aggregates, 74; *see also* creation
Diagoras, 84-5
dialectic, 11, 55, 87, 106-7; *see also* logic
Diogenes Laertius, 15, 27, 111, 139
doxographers, doxographical tradition, 14-15, 18, 37, 69

Earth, element of, 23, 28, 44, 60, 63, 107-9, 119
earth: equilibrium of, 26; shape of, 26, 38, 121; movement of, 38-9
education, 11, 33, 80-1; Socratic, 88, 93; Platonic, 95, 96, 102; of women, 103; *see also* gymnastics, music
Egypt, 11, 17, 18, 19, 21, 29, 38, 140, 152
Elea, 49, 50, 55, 72

171

Index

Eleatic School, 49, 58

elements, 20; in Empedocles, 60-1, 63; as 'seeds', 69; as 'letters', 74; in Plato, 107-9; in Aristotle, 119, 121, 122

emotion, Stoics on, 136-7

Empedocles, 59-65; life, 59-60; writings, 60; and Parmenides, 60; pluralism, 60-1; on change, 61; on perception, 61-2; on world process, 62-4; on soul, 64-5; Aristotle on, 121

empiricism: in Aristotle, 114-15, 130; in Stoics, 133

Enlightenment, Greek, 79

Epictetus, 139

Epicureanism, Epicurus, 11, 131-2, 139-48, 149; sources, 14; and Democritus, 73; life, 139-40; writings, 139-40; physics and cosmology, 141-2; on soul, 142-4; ethics, 144-6; on society, 146; on friendship, 146-7; on religion, 147; and Sceptics, 149

epistemology, *see* knowledge

ethics, 9, 11; in Heraclitus, 47-8; Sophistic, 82-3; Socratic, 91, 93; Platonic, 104; Aristotelian, 113, 123-9; Stoic, 132-3, 135-9; Epicurean, 144-8; *see also* virtue

Fire, element of, 23, 24, 28, 44-5, 60, 63, 107-9, 119

form: Pythagoreans on, 39; Aristotle's concept of, 118-19, 127, 130

Form of Good, 101-2, 107

Forms: in Plato, 99-102; terminology of, 99; nature of, 99; as cause of qualities, 100; as ideal patterns, 100; ascent to, 105; recollected by soul, 105-6; and dialectic, 106-7; as world model, 107

friendship, 95, 146-7

geometry, 18-19, 38, 102, 106, 108-9

Gnostics, 153, 159, 160

God, gods, 12-13, 22, 29, 30, 35, 50, 63, 68, 82, 84-5, 106; a mortal as god, 59; mystical union with, 105, 153, 155; as Maker and Father, 107-8; World as a god, 108; as particular, 117; as pure Form, 118; in Aristotle's theology, 122-3; in Stoicism, 134; in Epicureanism, 142, 147; as the Good, 155, 158; *see also* religion, theology

Good, as first principle, 101-2, 107, 155

good, of individual, 90-1, 123-5; of society, 124, 137-8

Gorgias, 80, 84

gymnastics, gymnasia, 33, 87, 95, 96, 111

happiness, 123-5, 129, 135, 136, 145, 149-50

Hellenistic Age, 11, 131, 149

Heraclitus, 32, 36, 40-8; life, 40-1; writings, 40-1; *logos* of, 41-2; on opposites, 42-3; on world process, 43-5; on flux, 45-6; on intelligence, 46; on soul, 46-7; and Parmenides, 53, 54; and motion, 62

Homer, 12, 35, 46, 50

homoeomereity, 69-70

homosexual love, 94-5

idealism, 12; in Plato, 99; in Plotinus, 152, 158-9

Ideas, *see* Forms

immortality, 129; denied by Epicurus, 144; *see also* soul

indeterminate, substance, 23-4; *see also* matter

infinity, infinite divisibility, 56-8, 70-1

intelligence, intellect, 46, 47, 77; and the virtues, 90, 128-9, 155; *see also* mind

Ionia, geography, 16; early history, 16-18, 22, 27; religion and culture in, 29-30; spirit of, 50

Ionians, 17; in exile, 23, 32-3, 49

justice: cosmic, 25, 45, 46, 63; human, 104, 146

Justinian, 10, 96, 160

knowledge, 10, 11; and reality, 52; Atomists on, 76-7; and virtue, 90-1; Plato on, 99, 100; and perception, 114-15; Stoics on, 133-4; Sceptics on, 149-51

law: rule of, 17, 40, 47; of nature, 45; evolution of, 85; 'natural', 138; *see also* justice (cosmic)

Leucippus: life, 72; writings, 73, 76; inventor of Atomism, 73-4; cosmology, 75-6

life: and water, 20-2, 47; breath of, 28-9; kinship of all, 35; Form of (Plato), 108; divine, 123; in Plotinus, 156-7

logic, 9; development of: by Socrates, 89; by Aristotle, 112; by Stoics, 133; *see also* argument, dialectic

logos, 42, 47, 119, 157, 164

Love, as cosmic force, 62-4; Plato on, 95; love of beauty, 105, 159

Lyceum, 111

magnetic attraction, 21-2

Marcus Aurelius, 14, 137

mathematics, 9, 11, 29; in Pythagoreanism, 37-8, 39; in Academy, 93; in Plato, 101, 106, 109; *see also* geometry

matter, 22, 24; Anaxagoras on, 68-71; particulate view of, 78; Plato on, 108, 109; Aristotle on, 118-19, 120; in Stoic physics, 134; Plotinus on, 157-8

medicine: in Near East, 29; Greek, 33

Melissus, 72, 73

memory: training, 34; of Forms, 105; in Aristotle, 114; in Stoics, 133

metaphysics, 9, 11; rejected, 84, 101, 113; *see also*

172

Index